Journeying Together

Growing youth work and youth workers in local communities

Edited by

Alan Rogers and Mark K. Smith

Russell House Publishing

First published in 2010 by:
Russell House Publishing Ltd.
4 St. George's House
Uplyme Road
Lyme Regis
Dorset DT7 3LS
Tel: 01297-443948
Fax: 01297-442722
e-mail: help@russellhouse.co.uk
www.russellhouse.co.uk

British Library Cataloguing-in-publication Data:
A catalogue record for this book is available from the British Library.

ISBN: 978-1-905541-54-6

Typeset by TW Typesetting, Plymouth, Devon

Printed by Page Bros, Norwich

Russell House Publishing

Russell House Publishing aims to publish innovative and valuable materials to help
managers, practitioners, trainers, educators and students.
Our full catalogue covers: social policy, working with young people, helping
children and families, care of older people, social care, combating social exclusion,
revitalising communities and working with offenders.

Full details can be found at www.russellhouse.co.uk and we are pleased to send
out information to you by post. Our contact details are on this page.

We are always keen to receive feedback on publications and new ideas for future
projects.

Dedicated to

Fred Arthur Rank Packard – Rank Foundation Trustee 1986–2009, Chairman 2000–2009

The Honourable Mrs S. M. Cowen ('Toddy') – Rank Foundation Trustee 1972–2000

and

Sue Bennett – Key worker/*Investing in Success* Initiative (2003–2006)

Jane Caley – *Youth or Adult?* Worker (1987–92) and Manager

David Clements – Manager *Youth or Adult?* Initiative (1992–97 and 1999–2004)

Carl John – *Youth or Adult?* Worker (1992–97) and Manager

Journeying together

Contents

Journeying together

Acknowledgements

The editors and contributors would like to thank the managers and workers from the Rank Charities youth work initiatives who were involved in workshops, meetings and explorations associated with the making of this book, and the students of the YMCA George Williams College who have also been involved.

Contributors

Zareena Abidi-Sheldon has worked for many years with young people around entrepreneurship and business. She has also been a worker and a manager within the *Youth or Adult?* Initiative and a distance learning tutor for the YMCA George Williams College since 2004.

Chris Dunning is Director of Youth Projects in Scotland for the Rank Foundation. He previously held posts in the fields of outdoor development training, youth work and teaching.

Charlie Harris is Director of Youth Projects in England and Wales for the Rank Foundation.

Simon Hill was a worker within the *Youth or Adult?* Initiative and has set up and managed a project training gap year students in Bournemouth. He has recently relocated to Durham with his wife Claire and their baby boy.

Alistair Hunter is currently a Tutor and Development worker for the YMCA George Williams College and was, for 12 years, Chief Executive of Kinetic in Fife.

Jon Jolly is a community-based youth worker and manager in Littlehampton, West Sussex. He is a graduate of the *Youth or Adult?* Initiative and regularly writes for youth work publications.

Sarah Lloyd-Jones is manager of the People and Work Unit, an independent charity that works across Wales undertaking evaluation and research work for public bodies and runs it own action-research projects in South Wales. The Unit works with young people in community settings, working in partnership with local groups and organisations.

Gemma McDonald is a youth development worker for a third sector agency in the North East. She completed the *Youth or Adult?* Programme in 2006, and is still loving every minute!!!!

Alan Rogers is a consultant, writer and editor in the field of youth and community work. He edits *the Source* – UK Youth's online magazine.

Jeff Salter is a Senior Lecturer at the YMCA George Williams College. He is also the Rank Tutor and Distance Learning Programme Organiser for Teaching and Staffing and has previously worked in the voluntary and statutory sectors as a youth worker, manager and teacher.

Judith Skinner is Outreach and Development Manager at the YMCA George Williams College. She has been a youth worker in both the voluntary and statutory sectors and has been involved in a number of Rank Foundation Initiatives.

Mark K Smith is the Rank Research Fellow and Tutor at the YMCA George Williams College. He edits *infed.org* and his recent books include *Informal Education* (with Tony Jeffs) and *The Art of Helping Others* (with Heather Smith).

Kai Wooder is the Education Manager for the sexual health charity, Wirral Brook. She enjoys facilitating group work and personal development training.

Foreword

Charlie Harris, Director of Youth Projects,
The Rank Foundation

How do you begin a foreword to a book that documents a significant part of your life's work and commitment? The roots of the *Youth or Adult?* Initiative – and the routes that led to its inception – go back six decades, not just (!) the 22 years it has been operational.

Youth or Adult? – which has now grown to become the Rank Youth Workers' Apprentice Programme (YAP) – is the longest and largest running initiative of its sort in the UK. For 22 years it has supported grass roots developmental youth and community work, alongside the professional training and qualification of its leaders.

The philosophy that underpins *Youth or Adult?* goes back to the Stone Age of my own education – certain role models, certain teachers and their educational approach. It goes back to my learning at the 'Central School of Screech and Trauma'. The brilliance of its take on education was founded on a sense of 'community' – and the understanding that creativity is a powerful tool and change is not a threat.

From 'Central' I went on a journey, through community development, play and youth work. Along the way I recognised the pragmatic value of investing for the long-term.

Education and experience liberate. Education should focus on potential. It explores the power of alternatives to the mire of despondency and shows a path through the wilderness. The investment is the essential catalyst, initiating an essential fusion and releasing a gigantic energy source.

In the mid 1980s, the right dynamic people were in the right place at the right time. The Rank Foundation and The Joseph Rank Trust were willing and keen to invest in leadership for the future. It was the beginning of a close partnership between the two bodies, the fruits of which are sampled within these pages. The investment would be nominally for five years but, for community and young people, it was actually investing for a lifetime – as qualification and professional commitment don't disappear like steam.

From the Welsh Valleys to the highlands of Scotland there are community leaders I would trust with the care of my grandchildren. That is *my* definition of 'qualification'. So, let the Journey continue, let's reach out for the myriad of bright stars and beyond.

Introduction

Charlie Harris, Alan Rogers and Mark K Smith

This is a unique collection of writings on work with young people. The 10 Chapters have grown from almost 25 years of work with a consistent youth work philosophy. They combine to set out a vision for effective work with young people in communities, which will be relevant to anyone working, or training to work, with young people.

Our aim in compiling this collection is to offer an accessible and authoritative account of an effective approach to growing work within communities. Quotes telling the stories of practicing youth workers and their managers are linked to established theories of practising organisational and community development.

The book

Journeying Together both articulates and evidences the nature and success of the approach to work with young people that the Rank Foundation's *Youth or Adult?* programme has supported throughout its existence. Collectively, the Chapters identify models of youth and community work practice, personal and professional development – and of funding practice. They combine to give a vision of community development, based on current practice.

The three sections . . .

Growing youth work in local communities: An analysis of the nature of informal education; the importance of youth work rooted within communities and the challenges this brings.

Growing youth workers in local communities: It takes special people to be informal educators with young people. Growing the skills, confidence and experience to be an effective youth worker is the central challenge for workers and their managers.

Journeying together: A commitment to a genuine partnership, involving the funders, the training agency and local organisations is at the root of the success of Rank's *Youth or Adult?* programme. All parties contribute to the growth of the workers-in-training at the centre of the process. And all partners grow through their collaboration.

The ten chapters . . .

The writers are practitioners – workers, managers, trainers and funders – who are actively involved in growing innovative work in local communities. Most of the writers have come (or are coming) through the *Youth or Adult?* process of growing their skills as workers in communities.

There is no standard approach to the chapters – all grow from personal experience, reflecting a philosophy that encourages and facilitates locally defined problems and solutions.

The research for the publication included interviews and workshops with workers and managers of current and past projects from across the Rank Network. Quotations from this process are included throughout the publication and are indicated by italicisation in the text.

The conclusion

In the conclusion, Alan Rogers and Mark Smith examine some of the wider implications of this unique strand of work with young people. The focus is on the challenges faced by local agencies, policy-makers and funders.

An approach to youth work . . .

During the lifetime of The Rank Foundation's *Youth or Adult?* programme, many government initiatives have come and gone. For more than two decades, however, *Youth or Adult?* has had the same, simple idea at its core – and the same values underpinning its practice at all levels.

In essence, *Youth or Adult?* offers individuals the opportunity to work within their community, while receiving professional training as informal educators. The goal is to grow workers and organisations that are able to make a sustained and sustainable impact on their communities. After over two decades there is plenty of evidence of personal, professional, organisational and community development to illustrate the success of this approach.

Since its inception, the programme has grown – and complementary initiatives have been built around it. The intertwining of structured training with 'real' work experience is distinctive and is built on a vital partnership between the Foundation and The YMCA George Williams College. But the goal of the programme is not the whole story. What makes it distinctive is how the underlying values have guided practice at all levels.

The Rank Foundation's vision of youth work is clear. Youth work:

- Trusts young people – based on a fundamental belief that there is good in all.
- Facilitates relationships that allow young people to grow and flourish.
- Creates space for the chance to reflect, learn and grow.
- Enables opportunities to join together to organise and take part in groups and activities.

These ideas are expanded in the DVD and booklet '*Journeying together*' [available online at www.rankyouthwork.org].

... and youth work funding

The Foundation has aimed to grow a way of working in partnership that is consistent with its ideas about good youth work practice.

As funders of youth work, this means:

- Listening to the plans of workers and agencies, rather than defining their targets.
- Regular personal contact with trainees and their managers.
- Regular opportunities for contact and learning with and from others involved in the programme.
- The growth of a network of funded individuals and projects, providing mutual support.

In summary, funders, trainers, agencies and individuals are 'journeying together' and learning together about how to support and grow skilled and experienced workers in communities.

Using this approach, local solutions are devised through dialogue. Workers and organisations initiate projects and programmes that meet local circumstances, rather than being obliged to use strategies imposed by a distant funder. This way of working means that both change and diversity are desirable and sought, rather than problematic.

Since 1987 just over 200 agencies have hosted a Rank Charities' funded *Youth or Adult?* project. Tens of thousands of young people have benefited from the Initiative – and through support from the other funding strands that have grown around it. Within *Youth or Adult?* alone, around 135 workers have qualified as professional workers, another 40 are currently undergoing training to degree level. Through the Rank Foundation's wider funding programme a further 90 workers have achieved recognised qualifications and 950 volunteer leaders have been grown. What is more, it has created a body of innovatory, local work with young people. Alongside this, there has been significant development, both in the size and shape of the organisations involved and the depth and range of work they are undertaking.

The 'journeying together' approach has contrasted increasingly with mainstream approaches to funding, especially with government funding strategies, which have increasingly sought to define targets and outcomes for local agencies to achieve. It has, to some degree, 'swum against the tide'. However, as the evidence of these pages shows, there has never been a time when the lessons from this journey have been more widely relevant.

Growing youth work in local communities

CHAPTER 1

Local youth work

Jon Jolly

> *Learning gets passed on. You can't help it. A young person gets some training, becomes a youth worker and then starts the cycle again with other young people. It's just how youth work – works!*

This chapter introduces the idea of local youth work. I begin by clarifying the meaning of the term 'youth work', before looking at how it grows and flourishes in a local setting.

My aim is to present the case for the importance and benefits of growing locally-based youth work and youth workers.

I became a youth worker almost by accident. I had been looking for a job in the town where I grew up and saw an advert for a part-time worker at a local youth project. Although I had done some voluntary work with children and had attended a youth club as a teenager, I had no real idea of what youth work entailed. Still, I went for an interview and to my surprise was given the job.

Over those first few months I found myself getting to know a core group of young people, taking them on outings, visiting homes, wandering the streets and learning a great deal.

Now, many years later, I realise that my own experience of starting out in youth work is far from unique. Growing youth work (and youth workers) in local communities is a common occurrence:

I joined a church small group as a teenager and really liked the environment. After a while I got asked to help out with one of the groups. I found that I loved it and it wasn't long before I became a youth worker!

Later, I will argue that these locally-based youth workers are essential to the success of youth work. However, before we explore that debate, we need to be clear about what we mean by youth work.

Defining youth work

Many diverse clubs, activities and ways of working with young people are commonly described as examples of 'youth work'. From traditional youth clubs and uniformed groups, like the Scouts, to detached work, work in schools, organised sports activities and more. The sheer variety of work with young people makes it very difficult to identify common ground.

The National Occupational Standards for youth work, updated by the National Youth Agency and Lifelong Learning UK in 2008, provide a starting point for trying to define what is common to good youth work practice. The document includes a statement that defines the key purpose of youth work. It is to:

Enable young people to develop holistically, working with them to facilitate their personal, social and educational development, to enable them to develop their voice, influence and place in society and to reach their full potential.

LLUK, 2008: 3

There is some useful information here: the terms 'young people', 'educational' and 'society' give some hints towards its focus. However, while this statement contains part of the puzzle, it does not give us a clear picture of the nature of the work. For example, *how* is youth work able to develop young people holistically? And what differentiates it from other educational disciplines?

To fully understand what youth work is we need to examine some common characteristics in its practice, rather than rely on general statements in isolation. Jeffs and Smith (2010: 4–6) identify five characteristics that form the foundation of youth work practice and provide a purpose to the work. Over the next few pages I will draw upon these five characteristics, explaining their importance and interdependence.

1. There is a focus on young people

Given the term – 'youth work' – it should come as no surprise that it is concerned with young people! But the title does beg a more important question: why has work with young people developed as a specialist activity?

According to Savage (2007) young people view their experiences as being different to other age groups; they also seek out each other's company. We know, both from personal experience and biological study, that the period of adolescence and puberty is a unique time of change and transition, where a young person starts to test and form their own sense of identity (first proposed by Erikson, 1995: 211). As a consequence of the internal changes and the way in which they view themselves, young people can perceive the world differently to those of other ages. It is a distinctive feature of youth work: to provide a suitable response to those experiences.

Youth work aims to respond creatively to the needs of young people in a way that is appropriate and relevant to them.

> We recently started up a girls' group, in response to what the young people were telling us. There are a lot of boys' activities locally, but there was nowhere for girls to come and talk about the issues affecting them. Now they have that space and we're busy getting to know them all and supporting them with their concerns.

The challenge of working with youth, therefore, requires workers to understand and respond to the particular needs and experiences of this age group (Jeffs, 2001: 156). However, the term 'youth' itself can be very difficult to define. Different agencies have differing criteria to define who they will – or will not – work with.

In addition, evidence suggests that adolescence is lengthening, due to rapid 'changes in technology, economics, culture, politics, demographics, the environment, and education' (Lloyd, 2005: 17). This is leading to a widening in the definition of those classed as 'youth'. Regardless of individual definitions, there is underlying agreement that a transitional period of 'youth' remains distinctive.

2. Young people choose to be involved

Youth work is not an enforced activity; it is about working with young people on their own terms. Young people do not *have* to go to a youth activity; they can decide whether or not they would like to join in. This idea of voluntary participation distinguishes youth work from other disciplines (Jeffs, 2001: 156).

Another aspect that makes youth work, as we define it, distinct is that it allows young people the freedom to choose when and where they want to engage in activities and relationships with youth workers. Increasingly, most other activities for or with young people are compulsory. Whether it is school, probation services or targeted projects, young people are required by law, or coerced by adults, to participate.

The ultimate control of a youth work activity is with the young people. An individual may decide to attend a youth club for a day, a week or a number of years – it is down to them. Voluntary participation also allows young people to be able to choose when they want to end these relationships or disengage from activities – they can vote with their feet! This can be problematic for workers, as there can be no certainty over the length of time young people might be involved. Instead, a worker must rely on their skills to engage young people and keep them interested in participating.

3. There is a concern with learning and well-being

Many may assume that youth work developed simply to give young people things to do – activities that would stop them causing problems for other members of society. In reality, however, youth work holds a strong tradition of providing welfare services and education for young people. It is motivated by a concern for the opportunities available to young people.

What we now call 'youth work' grew out of a desire to help and educate. The early history of the work is linked to Sunday schools that sprung up in churches in the late 18th century, which worked informally to provide Bible reading and basic skills to those who attended (Sutherland, 1990: 126). By the mid 19th century, ragged schools were educating young people 'in far from ideal settings like stables, under railway arches, church halls and run-down houses' (Smith, 1999).

As society began to recognise adolescence as a particular life stage, with its own needs and issues (greatly helped by G. Stanley Hall's (1904) influential work) specific youth institutions began to form. There are various examples of early youth agencies that provided services such as food, clothing, basic health care, and even financial support, in addition to activity and community.

I love the job that I do. We give accommodation to vulnerable young adults, providing places for them to live and stay and be independent. It allows them to learn how to be an adult and how to cope with all those things. I love making a difference to their lives in this way.

Although the government today provides most mainstream welfare and educational services in the UK, youth work is still significantly involved in supporting young people. Usually, this is through informal and relational methods that are difficult for more formal state services to utilise. As such, youth agencies continue to provide advice and information on issues relevant to young people, such as careers, sexual health, and accommodation, amongst others.

The concern with education is still central. While it might be unusual to see a maths class take place in a youth club, workers constantly use informal methods to encourage learning. Examples might include using outdoor activities to build cooperation and esteem, or planning a celebration event as a tool to advance organisational and interpersonal skills among a group.

4. Cooperation, community and belonging are encouraged

The term 'association' is perhaps one that is not commonly understood or used in everyday talk, yet it has always been a defining aspect of youth work practice. Association is about individuals coming together for a purpose, allowing them to take part in a larger group or organisation (Doyle and Smith, 1999: 44) as in the example below:

> The teenagers at the club were really keen on skateboarding but there was nowhere locally. They decided to petition the local council and with help from our youth agency, organised meetings, events and surveys over a number of months learning valuable skills along the way. There was a real sense of achievement and belonging amongst the group.

Many clubs and activities provide a setting to meet and make friends with people. They facilitate association almost accidentally through an environment of cooperation and participation, where members feel valued and included. These sorts of groups help to provide a sense of community for young people. This idea of 'community' is of central importance to youth work as it 'plays a crucial symbolic role in generating people's sense of belonging' (Crow and Allan 1994: 6).

5. The personality of the worker is vital

The first four characteristics of youth work help to give us a good sense of the nature of youth work. It is focused on young people, they choose to be involved, there is a strong concern for education and welfare, and youth work encourages cooperation and belonging. However, these only really make sense together when appreciated through the fifth characteristic: the youth *worker*. It is no exaggeration to say that the single most important factor in defining youth work practice rests with the worker.

There is a general expectation in youth work that workers should get on well with, and be liked by, young people. It makes sense. Most of us can think fondly of adults who encouraged or inspired us when we were younger. They may have been a teacher, family friend or youth worker, but they held a certain rapport with us and earned our respect:

> *At the youth club where I work, we constantly get adults dropping in to ask for the previous club leader. Although he has since retired, he ran the club for over twenty years and was so highly regarded by the young people who attended that they all come back to see him.*

The example is not uncommon. There is something about the way these adults accept young people, and the fact that young people choose to be around them. Basil Henriques suggests that the success of any youth club rests 'upon the personality and ingenuity of the leader' (Henriques, 1933: 60).

With success dependent on their own character, youth workers face the interesting challenge of working in relaxed and informal ways to attract young people to their activities – or going to the places where young people already are. While equipment and resources may initially draw young people to an activity, their continued involvement rests upon the worker's ability to engage with the young people.

> *We were doing a tidy up of the youth centre on a Saturday morning. It was going to be a long and miserable task. Although we'd asked the young people to help us, I wasn't expecting anyone to turn up. To my surprise, within half an hour, six of our members arrived ready to get stuck in!*

In this example, even though there was a potentially difficult and uninspiring task, the young people chose to attend and help the worker. There was no reward or incentive involved. The relationship the worker had developed with the group encouraged both belonging and participation.

We have already seen that youth work places a high value on building relationships, as it encourages association and belonging. When appreciation and trust develop in a relationship, there is a basis for learning – another characteristic of youth work. As Rogers (1967: 305) states, 'The facilitation of significant learning rests upon certain attitudinal qualities that exist in the personal relationship between facilitator and learner'.

At a basic level, it can be argued that every relationship involves some kind of exchange between people (Goetschius and Tash, 1967: 137). The role of a youth worker is to develop this exchange into something more meaningful that goes beyond everyday contact to become 'more appreciative of and receptive to the other's perspective' (Tiffany, 2001: 95). In this way, the worker is ultimately responsible for facilitating learning through their relationship with young people.

Core values

No two youth workers are the same, so we cannot easily pin down specific character traits or personality types to explain how these people are able to effectively engage and work with young people. Each has their own skills, strengths, ideas, beliefs and methods of working.

Yet, despite the differences, there are some core values that most youth workers embody. These values inform the way they work with young people and the choices they make. They define how they react to problems and how they inspire and encourage others.

Every worker has to make difficult decisions and the outworking of these values can be problematic, as the worker has to balance their own beliefs and values against those of others.

The core values of youth work are notoriously hard to define and often open to debate and interpretation, yet Jeffs and Smith have made an initial starting point. They are; 'Respect for persons, the promotion of well-being, truth, democracy, fairness and equality' (Jeffs and Smith, 2005: 35). These values are explored further and exemplified throughout this publication.

Being local

Now that we have a better understanding of what youth work entails and the significance of the worker in facilitating it, we shall explore the importance of being grounded locally in established good practice.

We must first define what we mean by the term 'local'. We have already used the word 'community' to describe the sense of belonging and association that youth work can foster in people (Crow and Allan, 1994: 6) yet 'community' is also widely used to refer to a specific place. In everyday conversation, we generally take, 'local', to mean a particular geographical area around where we live, work or visit. It is about proximity to us. There are local shops, local people and a local community. In this section we will be primarily using the idea of place, when talking of 'being local' and 'community'.

Local workers

At the beginning of the chapter, I described how I got involved with youth work in my home town. If I'm honest, I was surprised that I was given the job, as I had very little experience of working with young people professionally. However, I did have a great advantage over the other candidates: my local knowledge! Having grown up in the area, I already understood the issues and tensions affecting the community and was able to relate well to people. I knew the area well, could find my way around certain streets, knew where the young people went after school, and many other little bits of information that you pick up from living in an area for a long period of time.

Although, at the time, I was not conscious of this particular ability, my employers knew that I was well placed to connect with the local young people and build relationships. As Geertz (1983: 168) argues that education 'works by the light of local knowledge' and I was local!

'Home-grown' workers often get involved in youth work as a helping hand, to fulfil a particular need, such as coaching a sports team, running the snack bar or driving a minibus. Over time, many end up leading or developing the work:

> I got involved because I was too old to continue going to the club. I would come back to help with certain activities and ended up getting training and leading some groups!

It is within this local context that youth work really thrives! Despite the recent 'professionalisation' of youth work by the government and a shift towards more outcome-driven work among the statutory sector (DfEE, 2002) youth work has always been largely run and maintained by voluntary workers and organisations (NYA, 2007: 2). The vast majority of youth work is run by local volunteers in various clubs, groups and organised activities.

There are many advantages to this 'localised' approach. McLaughlin and colleagues (1994: 5) found that locally-grown youth work tends to have a better understanding of the needs of the area, is able to be responsive to local concerns, and is more highly regarded by those who use its services.

> Working in a smaller area, it's easier to form relationships and bonds with people. If you come from outside, the barriers go up and people don't trust you.

When something is defined as local, close and familiar, other things have to be 'outside', distant and unfamiliar. There is an invisible, flexible boundary that dictates what is 'in' and what is 'out' (Cohen, 1985: 12). This perception changes between individuals, groups and places: a person from a particular community might refer to a certain pub as their 'local', because it is the closest to their home, while their neighbour might choose to frequent a more distant pub, because of the social opportunities it provides them. 'Locality' is subjective.

Workers recognise that it can be harder to build trust and relationships, when you are perceived as 'outside' of the local. This causes a potential dilemma for youth workers who do not live in the community where they work, as they must try to understand the complex issues of a community from the 'outside'. Larry Parsons commented on this issue, noting that 'to be a credible role model to whom others can relate, it is necessary to share the conditions in which members of the group have to live' (Parsons, 2002: 10).

There are also issues for 'local' workers. Home-grown youth workers will 'still have the task of gaining acceptance as workers, rather than as neighbours, as family or as friends' (Smith, 1994: 15). They have to overcome how they are already perceived by the community, in order to gain respect in their role. This process of gaining acceptance and developing relationships can be a long one:

> When I first started at the youth project, there was a particular young man who I knew had been through very difficult family circumstances. My manager had told me a little bit of information about the situation, yet this lad had never mentioned it to me directly. Although I worked with him every week on various activities, it was only after **four years** that he decided to tell me about his past. I never asked him a question or prompted the discussion, he just felt finally able to trust me.

In the example above, it took four years for the worker to become fully accepted by that young person. But acceptance is not the only issue facing workers who come from their own neighbourhoods. It is also possible that locally-grown workers may not have either the experience or a wider perspective that will help them develop both themselves and their work with young people.

It can be very easy to get caught up in the customs and habits of a community without critically reflecting upon the reasons for doing so. These individuals may unintentionally limit their possibilities for 'emancipation and enlargement of experience' (Dewey, 1933: 340).

> When I started studying youth work, I was amazed at the wealth of theory around. For the first time, I could see that I wasn't alone in what I was

doing – people had done it, thought about it and come to some useful conclusions. It really helped to put my work in perspective.

There is a benefit to having a common experience of the community in which you work. Yet, it is still possible for a worker to be successful in their role if they come from outside a community. There are many examples of workers who have been 'adopted' by the area in which they work. The real importance is whether they are accepted and respected within the community. As we have seen, much of this depends upon their personality and ability to engage others.

Local organisations

However skilled a worker may be in fostering relationships and whatever rapport they have built with a community, they cannot work in isolation. The context in which the worker operates will also be of great influence. The advantages and disadvantages of being local are reflected at an organisational level.

Larger, perhaps national or statutory, agencies may well have a contract to 'deliver' youth work in a particular locality. Often these directives come with targets to achieve or a particular agenda to promote, such as the government targets around getting those young people who are Not in Education, Training or Employment (NEET) into some form of training or vocation (DCSF, 2008).

While the goal of wanting to offer young people opportunities is admirable, in practice it often involves workers operating across a wide geographic area and trying to encourage young people into one of their prescriptive outcomes, rather then seeking to build and foster relationships and belonging. A worker explains the dilemma:

Your motivation is different when you work for a larger organisation that is coming into an area. You care about the people but are there to do a job, not from a position of empathy or local understanding.

Conversely, smaller, locally established organisations are usually developed as a response to a particular need or issue in the community. They may flourish for a short time before finishing, or they may grow and develop new work, becoming a recognised part of the community life. These groups tend to run as local committees or charities, seeking funding to employ workers for the job that they do. They are often *ad hoc*, with little or no structure or finance. The big advantage of these organisations is that they are run by people who understand the community and its particular needs.

For the worker operating under a local organisation there is the potential of greater scope for creativity and freedom. In a study of local voluntary organisations in the UK, Elsdon et al. (1995: 47) found that there were significant positive benefits of these local groups:

The one which was given priority almost universally, and reported as being of greater importance than the content objective of the organisation, is quite simply growth in confidence, and its ramifications and secondary effects of self-discovery, freedom in forging relationships and undertaking tasks, belief in oneself and in one's potential as a human being and an agent, and ability to learn and change both in the context of the organisation's objectives and in others.

Civil society

In addition to the benefits of engaging and inspiring young people, local youth work also has something else to offer the wider community: change. The idea of voluntary involvement where people and organisations provide good-will services for the benefit of others is often called 'civil society' (Edwards, 2004).

Simply described, civil society is expressed through communal activity that exists independently from the dominating commercial and political agendas of our culture. It allows people the opportunity to express themselves by helping others for no reward. Any activity, such as visiting the elderly, running the Neighbourhood Watch group and serving on the school board of governors, are all forms of an engagement in civil society. Local youth work is a good example of this.

Research has shown that this sense of cooperation, belonging and 'shared life' is potentially much more empowering than simply helping people to feel good about themselves. Robert Putnam collected a range of compelling evidence to suggest that in places where trust and social interaction are strong, the individuals, businesses and general community tended to thrive economically (2000: 319–25). Essentially, it has been found that, where people actively engage in connecting with each other and working together, it can bring about significant positive change to the wider area.

'Connection' and 'working together' are essential factors for local youth work, where the participation and association of young people in the community is generated by the efforts and character of the worker. Not only is local youth work able to build relationships with young people to facilitate learning, but the transformative impact of this work can have a huge effect on the whole community!

Questions for reflection

- Did any adults influence your involvement in work with young people? ... what form did this influence take?
- What are the challenges for your work in demonstrating the first four characteristics of youth work – a focus on young people, voluntary involvement, a concern with education and well-being and encouragement of cooperation, community and belonging?
- What, in your experience, do young people respond to in the adults who work with them?
- How have you gone about gaining acceptance as a 'local' youth worker?
- In your experience, what is the value and impact of a locally managed organisation on the quality of life within a community?

CHAPTER 2

The experience of growing work

Sarah Lloyd-Jones

Youth work has traditionally been about working with young people in their own setting. It offered them the opportunity of somewhere within easy reach, where they could associate informally with their peers. Often hosted in local organisations, such youth work typically had strong links with particular communities and was part of civil society (Jeffs and Smith, 2010).

In the last 20 years, however, the focus has shifted away from community youth work towards issue-based work. This work seeks to address the 'problems' that young people present, with programmes set up to tackle, for example, anti-social or risky behaviour. Such work can be valuable, but in this chapter I argue that the challenges now facing young people mean that there is a greater need than ever for the role of generic, community-based youth work that gives young people the scope to explore who they are, rather than seeking to correct what they do.

A 'risk' society

Being young has never been easy but, arguably, the challenges facing young people now set particularly tough demands on youth work.

The second half of the twentieth century saw massive changes in social structures. The institutions that shaped and maintained social 'norms', including religion, state and family, lost their power, or will, to 'control' social and domestic behaviour. New opportunities developed for young people to define and construct their own identity. They were increasingly being seen less as a product of a predestined group or class and more as individuals. Policy has sought to support this (Margo and Dixon, 2006; Catan et al., 2004) with legislation to protect the right of the individual to make choices about how they wished to live and to remove social distinctions and prejudices.

As the century progressed it became easier for young people, it was argued, to move through the social class structure to the point where, by the end of the century, people were questioning whether the structure even existed any more (see Furlong, 1992). Migration continued to develop diversity within many communities; information technology opened up borders and allowed global understandings to develop with issues, such as environmental change and social justice, creating common causes across a world community.

In many ways, these new freedoms and tolerances have allowed for the development of a more inclusive and equal society. However, there are winners and losers in this analysis of the new world (Holtom and Lloyd-Jones, 2008) and something has been lost in the struggle for individual freedoms.

The positive impacts of social and economic change are not equally enjoyed by all young people and, it could be argued, they have not made people happier. A UNICEF report (2007) on child well-being, for example, ranked the UK bottom of 21 industrialised countries; we know that, in those societies with wide differentials between rich and poor, people tend to feel less happy (Wilkinson and Pickett, 2009). Ball et al. (2000) have argued that the 'new' urban economies, far from expanding opportunities, have generated new, and compounded old, inequalities. Such inequalities operate across *and within* communities.

The Good Childhood Report (Children's Society, 2009) illustrates how the focus on individualism has serious implications for many young people. It reports that children with single or step-parents, for example, are 50% more likely to suffer with lower academic achievement, poor self-esteem, unpopularity with other children, behavioural difficulties and depression. Family structures have become more varied and, whilst this shows how society has become more accepting of difference, it also represents greater instability in relationships.

There have been limitations put on the use of public space by young people, as can be seen through the growing privatisation of space through the development of malls and gated housing (Minton, 2009). On top of this, the economic crisis following the near collapse of the banking system in 2008 has disproportionately impacted on young people in the form of substantially increased levels of unemployment.

There was a 'safety' in the common experiences of living in a more externally controlled society for the majority (although minorities were always at risk). Young people were more likely to be provided with a set of common values and to know where the boundaries lay, even if it was only in knowing what to rebel against!

In today's society, individuals are expected to accept more responsibility for their own destiny, develop their own values and plan their own futures, all at an ever younger age. Common experiences have become individualised and transition to adulthood has become more personal, complex and extended, in the way it once was only for the academically successful (Catan, 2004). An increasing disparity has opened up between those young people who have access to resources that can help them navigate their way around education, training, social and employment options and those who do not. There is a link to poverty, since many of those resources come with affluence, and the gap between the poorest and the rest of society has grown wider, but even amongst the more affluent there are new and ever more complex pressures (Wilkinson and Pickett, 2009).

Beck (1992) writes about a 'risk' society in which, in order to prosper, young people need new types of competences that enable them to exploit opportunities. He argues that modernisation has created a new set of insecurities and hazards that are made by and managed through human agency (individual action and behaviour). The 'risk' society is a response to these 'manufactured' risks (Giddens, 1999) and illustrates how such risks affect everyone – and how their impacts are unevenly distributed across socio-economic classes.

The risks are based on what you know (or do not know) as much as what you do. For example, as the UK labour market places more focus on qualifications, making the right decisions on what to study in school is crucial. Some fourteen year olds know this; they have thought about it and made plans, so that when they have to make choices on courses to take they know what they are doing. Others have not, but have parents who are thinking about the future for them and guiding their decision-making. Still others have schools that 'manage' their thinking for them, making sure that they make the right choices. Young people who have none of these resources to guide their decision-making are at a real disadvantage.

For some young people, there is the additional pressure of navigating their way through competing sets of risks. There are risks, for example, in deciding to stay in school to get more qualifications, when a local social norm might expect you to leave at the earliest opportunity and look for a job. Deciding not to do what your friends are doing when you have no access to other social networks is a strategy that can leave someone very isolated. Bynner et al. (1997) and Jones (2002) write about how young people are constrained by factors beyond the control of the individual that conspire to create 'bounded agency' (Hodkinson, 1996; Evans et al., 2003). What we know, see around us and believe is possible controls how we respond to opportunities (Bourdieu,

1979). Class, poverty and poor education are still key factors in shaping that response. This can be seen in the way that the gap between the poorest and the rest of society has grown over the last few decades, with those at the bottom finding it increasingly hard to break the cycle of poverty and even being characterised by some as a new 'underclass' – seen either as victims of (MacDonald, 2002) or threats to (Murray, 1990, 1994) the rest of society.

If society, before the 1960s, could be characterised as 'too tight', demanding a level of conformity that confined young people to a predestined life shaped by class, locality and restrictive social norms, then society for *some* young people in the early twenty-first century could be described as 'too loose'. They are required to navigate their own way to economic and domestic independence with an inadequate social and moral compass to guide them and, at best, conditional and limited support.

Belonging

In the context of a 'risk' society, concepts of belonging take on a heightened meaning. People who feel distant from wider society will often be drawn to cultural norms that include them and provide a sense of belonging. Belonging helps people to feel connected to others, an essential prerequisite to maintaining healthy communities and personal well-being. Beynon et al. (1994) argue that *who* people are – their identity – is shaped by *where* people are.

Identity also comes from an understanding of the world (Cresswell, 2004; Geertz, 1983) a shared culture or faith. A sharing of values, experience and behaviour is comforting and offers a safe platform from which to contemplate new challenges.

Theories of social capital (Bourdieu, 1986) are built on an understanding of the impact of the influences on identity. Social capital theories offer a tool for understanding community (e.g. SQW, 2008) and the resources that young people can deploy to navigate their way through the 'risk' society. The theories argue that people are shaped by who they know; their interaction with other people works to build up social and cultural capital, which provides both status and the capacity to manage new experiences. There is a variety of interpretations of social capital and its role, but all recognise the importance of human relationships (Putnam, 2000; Field, 2008).

Working within the community

It is important to recognise that human relationships and the social capital they provide can constrain, as well as support, young people. At its worst, belonging to a community can lead to an embedding of disadvantage (see MacDonald and Marsh, 2005). This can be seen in the strong and enduring links between community, educational disadvantage and poverty (Kenway et al., 2005).

Problems arise when the values that are developed within a community are not transferable outside it. If we can describe social capital as the 'glue' that holds a society together (World Bank, 1999), we can see that it can also operate to 'trap' people in an area or community (MacDonald and Marsh, 2005). Johnston et al. (2000) write about how the tools young people develop in order to belong to a community can be the very characteristics that exclude them from broader society.

> The paradox is that local knowledge and plural networks are both a manifestation of Willowdene's separateness (its 'exclusion') vis-à-vis the wider area, **and a condition of existence of the social inclusion of residents within the locality**. Thus, while Willowdene possesses all of the official, objective indicators of social exclusion, the subjective experience of many young people growing up in the place – certainly those who are party to local knowledge and able to navigate local networks – is one of 'social inclusion'. Johnston et al., 2000: 23. *Authors' emphasis.*

Putnam (2000) and Kearns and Parkinson (2001) make a useful distinction in this context between 'bonding' social capital that helps people 'get by' within their community or socio-economic situation and 'bridging' social capital that helps people 'get on'. This distinction provides a valuable challenge to youth work, reminding workers that it is not enough for a young person to function effectively within the context of the group or club, the real test is how transferable the confidence is to other settings.

Understanding identity and belonging, then, provides a vital context for youth work and the basis for supporting young people to thrive in the risk society. Some young people see this understanding of their community context and the world vision it offers as an essential prerequisite to being able to work with them. If you do not understand who I am, they would argue, you cannot understand how to work with me. Simon, below, contrasts his experience of a primary school that he describes as rooted in his community, with the comprehensive, from which he was excluded at 14 years old and from which he felt disconnected because of its (physical and cultural) separation from his community. He saw respect and the basis of an effective teaching relationship as being predicated on an understanding of where he belonged.

Down in junior school, you was known by your first name, same with the infants – and they knew your family as well, so, like, it was alright. But then go up to comp and they are teaching so many – I think that's what it is, it's just that they are teaching so many people, they don't know people by their first names, they don't know what they are like, they don't know what their attitudes are like, and, it just goes downhill then, they lose respect for each other.

Lloyd-Jones 2005: 132

Like Simon, many young people place a high, although inconsistent, value on work and workers who share their experiences and culture. Outsiders can be seen as knowing little about 'real life' as experienced by *these* young people in *this* context. Consequently, they have to work harder to demonstrate that they have anything credible to offer.

The challenge for youth work is to recognise, and work (but not collude) with these limitations; to understand and work with them to enhance the strengths of belonging and mitigate the constraints. There is, for example, no stronger community than that of the addict, where those who share the habit can be very reluctant to see one of their number break free. A gang could also be described as a strong community. In both these circumstances a youth worker may need to understand the community but would want to challenge the conformity it demands.

The desire to belong, which leads to an imposition of limits linked to conformity (Green and White, 2007) and to a fatalism in young person and worker alike (*that is what happens here . . .*) operates to stifle personal and group development. Youth work offers, arguably, the unique opportunity to tackle these constraints at source by supporting young people to celebrate who they are and explore who they could be independently of where they belong.

A holistic approach

The strength of community youth work is that the continuity and holistic focus that it offers allows it to become part of a young person's social capital. It builds effective 'bonding' social capital by creating a safe environment. The setting becomes a context within which young people can explore the wider world and so develop the 'bridging' social capital necessary for meeting the demands of the 'risk' society. This is nothing new, it is an approach that has shaped youth work for over a century but, I would argue, never has it been more relevant or important than it is now in supporting young people in the 'risk' society.

Youth work is not a response to negative behaviours or the problems of an area, or any of the symptoms of dislocation. Rather it is a holistic offer of nurture and care that can provide the guidance, values and support that young people need, if they are to develop their capacity to manage risk, make decisions and take on responsibilities. This is the task that society needs youth work to focus on, if we are to stop condemning whole communities to a continuing cycle of poverty.

Community youth work offers the opportunity to work with young people's understanding and provides credible role models, who can impact on all young people. This has to be a genuine offer, though, and it is not one easily manufactured from outside. It has to be underpinned by a real respect for the community to which the young people belong, based on a thorough understanding of it.

The clear message from youth work agencies is that, to really understand a community, it is vital to listen to young people and what they define as their community, which may bear little resemblance to official boundaries. A dynamic and evolving understanding requires ongoing dialogue and re-assessment as things change. Objective, external ideas about, for example, how 'bad' an area is may not be reflected in local people's experience (Taylor, 2008; Lloyd-Jones, 2005; Green and White, 2007) and it is important to avoid making assumptions. Even local people can make risky assumptions based on their past experiences or a sub-set of the community they know: '*I used to know everyone around here but now I don't recognise half of them*' (youth worker talking about his home community).

When workers live within and/or develop effective relationships with the community they serve, the impact of not following through or keeping promises can be immediate and visible. In this way, quality control becomes about maintaining credibility and showing respect. Whether the community being worked with is one of locality, culture or faith, youth work should offer continuity, quality and a direct accountability. As one agency put it, '*we do what we say we will do*'. The credibility and relevance comes from the way that community-based work allows workers to be part of a young person's context and to make links with the families, friends, activities and schools that form part of their lives. The youth worker can see the whole person, the son, classmate, brother, friend, neighbour and father as well as the group member. In doing this, youth work can overlap with community work and provide opportunities for the young people involved to shape their community. As one local worker explained: '*when I started, youth work was very separate from community work – but now they have come together, there are much closer links*'.

There are discrete roles and purposes for agencies within a community and these need to be maintained to provide choice, but there is also a strength in cross-fertilisation. For example, a school can benefit from seeing a young person, who has 'behaviour problems' in the classroom setting, taking an active and positive role in youth and community work; this will suggest that the problem is not just the young person's, it could also be about the setting.

Relationships

Relationships are at the core of youth work (Goetschius and Tash, 1967; Davies and Gibson, 1967) and community youth work provides a strong environment for the development of relationships. A locally-based youth worker identified that *'the power of relationships is that they let you address needs'* and that working with young people in their own setting and from an understanding of their community was crucial to developing these relationships. Living in an area expands the type of knowledge a worker can gather about young people, allowing them to observe how life is lived as well as how it is presented:

> *I can react to how young people live their lives here, like when you are coming home from the pub after closing time and there are 13 year olds still on the streets.*
>
> locally based youth worker

The continuity of the work allows relationships to be built over time and ensures that, once developed, these relationships are precious and not easily abandoned. This means not giving up on participants when they do not attend; finding ways of working with those that do not respond well to what is being offered; working through reasons for withdrawal rather than accepting them; and recognising the competing demands on participants' attention and commitment. In this way, community-based work provides the opportunity to demonstrate coping and problem-solving behaviour and allows agencies both to support the development of social capital and to shape how it functions.

Relationships formed within the community provide scope to capture and nurture talent. Many youth work agencies have been able to support young people to achieve great things, including recruiting and qualifying their own work force from within the community. In many ways, these workers or leaders have a real advantage in establishing credibility (Smith and Smith, 2008). They provide a demonstrable example of how change can happen and have less to prove in terms of understanding the community they are working with. Bourdieu (1989) identified a form of symbolic capital that is of relevance here.

It provides a legitimacy and strength to an individual and is conferred by how that person is seen by others. Spillane (below) identifies how this symbolic capital works:

> When a potential leader possesses certain forms of capital **and** followers value them, followers attribute legitimacy to the leader based on these forms of capital. When this process of valuation and attribution occurs, the various forms of capital possessed by a leader are converted into 'symbolic capital', a measure of overall social esteem, a credit that can be deployed as symbolic power.
>
> Spillane et al., 2001: 5. Authors' emphasis

Workers who have backgrounds, skills or abilities that are recognised and given credibility within a community will attract symbolic capital from the young people with whom they work. This provides a strong base for developmental work.

Cross sector approach

Community-based work has the potential to coordinate and shape the services being offered by other agencies to meet those young people's needs. By taking a generic youth work approach, community agencies have been able to bring in and manage other services. In this way they are able to consolidate the work, when these services move on. They pull work together around needs, when other agencies often work in isolation. This role is possible because effective community youth work is essentially responsive, picking up on needs quickly and developing work around the concerns that young people prioritise. At its best, it offers the scope to exploit local networks and relationships to reach young people other services miss, recognising that each community will have specific needs because they are not all the same (Green and White, 2007).

Even within communities there are significant differences between people and their experiences. Gill Jones (2002) has identified how inequalities existing within communities can actually be overlooked by policies that take a holistic approach to community regeneration.

> Because social inequalities exist within communities, some people are more able to overcome community disadvantage than others. There are therefore dangers in focusing on communities, as targeted interventions may only help those who would have 'achieved' without them and fail to address the problems of others more in need (Jones, 2002: 41).

Good youth work seeks to manage factionalism within communities without further embedding it.

Limitations

Although community youth work has the potential to be a powerful tool in enabling young people to achieve change, it does not always succeed. Work that is developed by, with and for a community may showcase the strengths of that community, but can also share its limitations. If workers and leaders share the restricted experience, attitudes and aspirations of the young people with whom they work, they will fail to challenge assumptions and may further embed prejudice and the characteristics of exclusion.

There is a risk in forgetting to look outward as well as inward, in developing comfort zones but then failing to challenge and extend them. Kindermann (1996) found in his two studies of peer groups that young people tend to associate with those most like them in terms of their characteristics, skills and attitudes and that this has a reinforcing effect on attitudes, motivation and behaviour. Tackling this requires a sophisticated approach that balances achieving local credibility with using that credibility to expand horizons.

We have already explored how , in order to have credibility, those delivering the message need to be seen to know the communities young people belong to, since opportunities that ignore or dismiss the 'lived realities' (Rudd and Evans, 1998) of young people's lives can have no credibility and, consequently, no impact. Similarly, those who seek only to reflect young people's lives and are bounded by what is local and known will fail to make a real difference. Youth work needs, therefore, to be able to offer ideas and opportunities that are both visionary *and* rooted in an understanding of the individual's background and strengths.

All this shows that youth work is a dynamic and sophisticated discipline. It changes with young people as they develop and grow, expanding to meet new challenges with established participants, whilst also capturing the interests of new recruits. This mix of constancy and churn requires equal dynamism from leaders and workers as from the young people with whom they work. A manager's or worker's comfort zone has to develop as rapidly as the young people's.

Locally recruited staff, in particular, face the challenge of promoting change from within and the related pressure to be both 'one of us' and different (Doyle and Smith, 1999; Rank Foundation, 2008). This involves adopting a highly skilled and adaptive role that finds the balance between sharing the world vision of young people and expanding it to confront prejudice and intolerance and embrace new opportunities.

In addressing the danger of youth workers reflecting and sharing, rather than challenging, the limitations of localism, agencies identify two core strategies: one is to have a mix of locals and outsiders working with young people, ensuring that this team works together and develops a common vision, based on their various backgrounds and experiences. The other core strategy is training and investing in people as the key tool and resource that youth work has to offer. Not everyone can be a youth worker, but there are people in every community who have the heart and commitment to make a real difference to the young people around them. Providing these people with high quality training captures and shapes that natural aptitude into a professional youth work approach. Such training sets out to develop and expand their world view, making them a stronger and more powerful resource. Later chapters of this book will explore how training can impact on local workers and on the young people with whom they work.

Conclusions

It is not about going in to fix stuff – rather a long-term developmental process of cultural change.

youth worker

Life has, in many ways, become more complex and demanding for young people. There are higher expectations on them to operate as informed decision-makers, at a time when cultural guidance on what decisions to make has often been stripped away. As a result, they have to rely more than ever on the guidance of family and friends and on the social networks available to them. These social networks are largely shaped by local, cultural or faith communities and provide young people with some sense of belonging.

There are great strengths in the group identity and the shared values these communities offer. There are, though, also some weaknesses. Communities can have a limiting effect on a young person, encouraging them to look inward and conform to norms that deepen separation from the broader society. The power of these norms to shape young people is disproportionately seen amongst those young people who fail to thrive outside their community. For these young people, in particular, agencies lack credibility, unless they can acknowledge and work with the values and understandings they see within their community. And the agencies will lack impact, unless they can help young people develop these values and understandings to better reflect those needed outside that community.

Community youth work is uniquely placed to work with the social networks that young people draw on for their sense of belonging, whilst also challenging and expanding them. Its role is, arguably, more important than it has ever been in providing the opportunity for young people to develop the values, beliefs and strengths that will help them thrive in the risk society.

Community youth work is about a long-term investment, building relationships and credibility over time. This is youth work that starts by seeing young people as members of the community, within the context of the social networks and families and offers a safe setting to explore and challenge the values and beliefs embedded in that community. This means working alongside – but *neither with nor against* – the localism or community identity that underpins who they are. All this involves investing time in understanding what cultural values are embedded in the community and continually checking this understanding. It recognises communities as dynamic settings that change, sometimes rapidly.

Good community youth work is accountable to the young people with whom it works and to the communities of which they are part. Workers are reliable, keeping promises and connected. Credibility comes from being able to link understanding and beliefs from both within and beyond the community. Information and ideas come across as credible and realistic because they draw on community references. This does not mean that the information cannot challenge that understanding – merely that it has to be relevant to it.

Questions for reflection

- In your experience, has individualism worked to both promote equality and inclusion and embed inequalities?
- Do you agree that the need for youth work been heightened by the 'risk society'? If you do, what is it about the experiences of the young people you know or work with that has changed?
- As we have seen, there are considerable strengths in the group identity and the shared values local communities can offer. There are, though, also weaknesses. What has been your experience of this both as a member of, and a worker in, particular communities?
- In what ways could you develop work that explores and builds 'bonding' and 'bridging' social capital? What are some of the issues you could face?

CHAPTER 3

Developing local groups and organisations

Alistair Hunter

This chapter is a personal exploration of the power of local organisations and of what makes a 'successful' local organisation. It examine the key themes and organisational characteristics that, over more than a decade of youth and community work, I have observed lead to success at the front line of youth and community work.

In the following pages I use the generic term 'local organisation' to describe any locally-based agency, club or group. The material draws together themes and practices that are shared across organisations of all shapes and sizes.

The term 'successful' is used to capture the best practice that I have experienced. Part of the purpose of the chapter is to encourage people to reflect on their own organisation – and how they can influence it, as well as work within it.

Foreword: social capital

John Field (2008) has argued that the central ideas underpinning discussions of social capital are that social networks are a valuable asset and that relationships matter. He goes on to say that interaction enables people to build communities, to commit themselves to each other, and to knit the social fabric.

A sense of belonging and the concrete experience of social networks can, it is argued, bring great benefits to people.

> Trust between individuals thus becomes trust between strangers and trust of a broad fabric of social institutions; ultimately, it becomes a shared set of values, virtues, and expectations within society as a whole. Without this interaction, on the other hand, trust decays; at a certain point, this decay begins to manifest itself in serious social problems ... The concept of

social capital contends that building or rebuilding community and trust requires face-to-face encounters.

Beem, 1999: 20

Local organisations are at the heart of the creation of social capital. After identifying some defining characteristics of local organisations, this chapter will describe some of the key qualities that can help local organisations succeed in their goals. Finally, I outline my personal priorities for action by local organisations.

Being local

Local organisations have always played a fundamental role in developing individuals, groups and communities. By 'local organisations' I mean autonomous bodies and groups that work wholly or mainly for the benefit of the areas in which they are set up. In a modern world, where the social fabric of our communities is being stretched, the role of the local organisation has become more important than ever.

Kretzmann and McKnight say the purpose of an organisation is about 'empowering individuals (and groups), mobilising their capacities and working together'. They also describe the local organisation as being 'an amplifier of gifts, talents and skills of individuals, groups and communities' (1993: 109)

Community connections

Charles Handy argues that most organisations are not designed, they grow. He continues, 'but not all organisations adapt equally well to the environment within which they grow. Many, like the dinosaur of great size but little brain, remain unchanged in a changing world' (Handy, 1999b: 253). Successful local organisations have the ability to stay connected to their local communities and in touch with current and immediate trends. This is a very difficult task. It is, therefore, important that organisations have appropriate guiding principles in place.

The local organisation that I managed for a number of years, works with young people by maintaining a close, genuine and authentic relationship. As an organisation the values are learning, innovation, participation, empowerment and partnership. These values define the relationship with young people and also define how the organisation operates, how it grows, structures and delivers its purpose.

We expect young people's fashions, expectations and relationships to change on a regular (sometimes daily!) basis. Successful organisations, therefore, need to define their own purpose and organising principles using the same rules of engagement – they must master the ability to constantly reflect, understand and change!

Over the last 10 years this organisation has used a very simple strategy to develop a successful organisation. The strategy has two parts:

- Always work from the strengths of your client group.
- Always be prepared to give a practical demonstration of what you are proposing to do, in order to build trust and respect.

Local organisations must go on a shared journey with their communities and focus on what is important to them – successful local organisations are concerned with *practical solutions*.

Learning by doing

I am currently teaching my daughter how to ride her bike and spend long periods of time helping her to learn by doing. It is seemingly obvious that you can only learn to ride a bike by doing it. My daughter has to master the three basic principles of balance, steering and pedalling in order to be able to ride her bike. With my practical help and in her own time she has put all of the pieces together for herself and she will never forget.

I use this as an example because it highlights the simple yet practical 'can do' approach. If I had enlisted my local authority or government to do the job we would have assembled a committee to assess the situation; recruited people who understood the principles of balance, steering and pedalling. And finally we would have produced an extensive report with recommendations that formed a policy to be enacted to help my daughter ride her bike. The big picture approach would have no impact on her ability to ride a bike.

Local innovation

In the UK we are organised by and around the structures and arms of national and local government that have become fixated with political culture of blame and finding and fixing problems.

Local community organisations know intimately the long-term problems within their communities and are set the task of fixing them with short term financial and policy commitments. This approach has permeated youth work and I am constantly asked to talk to decision-makers and 'experts' who want to know why young people are involved in anti-social behaviour or why young people won't engage with services – both examples look for quick answers and in so doing are missing the point of appreciating the personal nature of the local organisation.

A parallel for this exists in the medical world where they have discovered that you don't learn about good physical health by studying illness, you learn about good health by exploring the reasons why people have good health. The same approach can be easily transferred back to youth work, young people and organisations, we must not be made to focus on anti-social behaviour cures or certificated achievement, instead we must focus on promoting *social* behaviour and the learning and skills agenda must be firmly based around the needs of the young person and not the solely economic or academic agendas.

In the last 10 years there has been an emerging breed of new, local organisations that mark a new direction for most charity-based, grant-receiving local organisations. These organisations have had a significant record of social innovation (Mulgan et al., 2007) and include a number of social enterprises. In the UK context, such social enterprises include community enterprises, credit unions, trading arms of charities, employee-owned businesses, co-operatives, development trusts, housing associations, social firms, and leisure trusts. Whereas conventional businesses distribute their profit among shareholders, in social enterprises the surplus tends to go towards one or more of the business' social aims – education, for example, vocational training or environmental issues.

Wider links

In our local communities local organisations are more likely to be connected to people, have their finger on the pulse and be aware of what is needed to bring about change. It is, therefore, essential that such agencies understand and have the ability to adapt to and work within the wider political, cultural and organisational environments.

As the physical and social assets within many local communities continue to break down, links to the wider world are critical. A vital function of local organisations is to connect with and influence the social, political and decision-making networks beyond the local community.

As local organisations we must be prepared to speak the many languages of partnership, embracing and delivering on our communities' and others' priorities to secure finance and ensure our communities' aspirations are furthered.

Crucially, we must find effective linking mechanisms that allow us to collaborate in a multi-faceted local world while protecting the integrity and honesty of our organisational and communities values. It is essential to understand the importance of bonding, bridging and linking with individuals, organisations, governmental entities and funding agencies.

Processes for success

This section of the chapter focuses on the processes that I have found within successful local organisations. I want to focus on mindset, envisioning and being resilient.

Mindset

Any organisation is made up of *people* working towards a vision. The organisation may have support mechanisms in place, such as values, aims, objectives, policies and procedures. But every individual within the organisation approaches those mechanisms with their own unique experience and personality.

The human factor has a major impact on the personality and culture of an organisation. It is essential, therefore, that we find ways to ensure that the human factor can be focused on building a healthy and successful organisation.

Carol Dweck has championed a simple and interesting theory that enables such an approach. She argues that people can be divided into two basic 'mindsets' and that these mindsets can be learned. She does not dispute that some people find some types of activities or learning easier than others, she disputes that others can't learn! Dweck's (2006) work is supported by substantive empirical research.

The fixed mindset

This mindset upholds the idea that people's ability is fairly fixed and not open to change. According to such a view, people are either 'sporty', 'academic', 'practical', 'musical', etc. or they aren't. This mindset also labels people according to personal characteristics. So people are either 'good' or 'bad', 'confident' or 'shy'.

The growth mindset

The growth mindset views people as adaptable. It suggests that they aren't fixed but have potential for development and growth. Dweck asserts that, with enough motivation, effort and concentration 95 per cent of the population can become better at almost anything. Dweck calls this the 'incremental theory', to suggest the idea that people are capable of making incremental changes in ability and other personal characteristics (Dweck, 2006).

This simple idea has massive implications for learning and how organisations can be shaped to make the most of their most volatile, yet important resources. Successful organisations and their people exhibit a 'growth mindset'. This mindset is acquired through recruitment of a certain type of individual and/or learned through induction, training and a conducive, working environment.

It is of critical importance to success that organisations and their leaders have a mechanism for understanding how staff think and how their thoughts can be orientated in a manner that is beneficial to the organisation. Many of us have witnessed the devastating effect that negative and fixed mindsets can have within teams and organisations and how quickly de-motivation or bad habits can spread due to an individual's approach.

Envisioning

Successful organisations are not just filled with positive people who are willing to develop themselves and grow; they are filled with people who believe in a vision and have a plan to create it. Applied strategic planning is defined as:

> The process by which the guiding members of an organisation envision its future and develop the necessary procedures and operations to achieve that future (Goodstein, Nolan and Pfeiffer, 1993: 38).

Collective vision

Creating a vision is a process that should involve all the stakeholders of an organisation. At a recent stakeholder day we refreshed our vision and mission statement and were blown away by the input of a 12 year old young person who gave an invaluable insight into his experience of working with the organisation.

Kouzes and Posner (2002) say that vision 'Provides an organisation with a forward looking, idealised image of itself and its uniqueness'. The direct input from this young man gave us the opportunity to drop all of the 'baggage' we had as staff, such as funding and office space, and focus on the truly important matters of our uniqueness as an organisation and what the future might look like.

Vision is only a part of the big picture: Joel Barker, a well-known futurist, shared his perspective by reflecting that:

... vision without action is merely a dream, that action without vision merely passes the time, but vision with action can change the world (Goodstein, Nolan and Pfeiffer, 1993: 39).

Enacting a vision needs a plan. Russell Ackoff (1981) suggests four ways that organisations plan for the future.

1. *Reactive*: planning through the rear view mirror.
2. *Inactive*: going with the flow.
3. *Preactive*: preparing for the future.
4. *Proactive*: designing the future and making it happen.

Being proactive

In my former organisation we made a concerted effort on proactive planning and have seen good results. We focused on understanding and setting out what we wanted the future for young people in the area to look like and how we would reconfigure all the parts of the youth work machine to make this happen.

The Street: The live programme which is the main focus of this plan has won two major awards in the two years since its inception and is being used by others around the country as a model of best practice – most importantly it is the most well attended youth provision in the whole area, because it is truly connected to young people.

Being 'resilient'

In recent years, the concept of 'resilience' has developed as a central pillar of positive psychology, which focuses on the empirical study of such things as positive emotions, strengths-based character, and healthy institutions. It differs from much existing psychological theory that pathologies emotions and aims to 'fix' or 'cure' problems or illnesses.

During a talk to the *Go Dundee* network Tal Ben-Shahar (2008) a leading positive psychologist and professor at Harvard, articulated resilience in the following terms. People and organisations who are resilient demonstrate the following qualities.

Goal focused

A central element of resilience echoes the importance of 'envisioning' and maintaining an orientation focused on the future. Local youth organisations must concentrate on 'delivering' on the needs and aspirations of young people and not be sidelined by the latest political whim or priority.

We are all too aware that resources follow centrally- and locally-set priorities and that we need resources to pay wages and other expenses. We must work to 'deliver' these priorities, while finding ways to realise them in a way that allows young people to be creative and fulfilled.

A key to success

When conducting an annual review and strategic plan, a new member of my former organisation's board reflected on the major difference he saw between successful and unsuccessful organisations. He said future orientated organisations exist to meet the needs of local young people and are happy to trust in young people and can shift their programmes to suit the ever-changing nature of young people.

Unsuccessful organisations need local young people to exist, so their needs can be met. They are scared of changing the *status quo*, because they have much to lose.

Seligman (2004) believes resilience theory rejects the idea that risk is something to be avoided. Instead, it focuses on those factors that promote well-being in individuals and organisations that are faced with adversity. He suggests that rather than take a defensive stance against risk, resilience theory takes the view that the life of an organisation, with all of its ups and downs, is there to embraced – and that coping with risk and bouncing back from adversity are good for the organisation and its success.

Positive role models and strong values

As organisations and educators, we have to 'walk the walk', not just 'talk the talk'. The following words (variously attributed to Rudyard Kipling, Arthur Gulterman and anon) explains why:

> No printed word, nor spoken plea
> Can teach young minds what they should be.
> Not all the books on all the shelves –
> But what the teachers are themselves.

During adolescence, young people are at their most vulnerable and impressionable age. They are in need of role models and take them from all areas that are close at hand, friends and family, board members, partners or mentors. The same applies to growing local organisations; in my many meetings with successful organisations, all can recall a pivotal time and set of experiences that have defined their approach and subsequent success.

Role models are not concerned with the imparting of knowledge and information. They demonstrate a specific set of values, attitudes, lifestyles and outlooks. Together, these form a frame of reference on which organisations (and young people!) make their choices. It is, therefore, critical to surround ourselves as individuals and organisations with role models who will add to a positive and constructive frame of reference (see Rose, 2004).

Focus on strengths

Successful organisations focus on strengths, the things that work for them and young people. They have strategies and approaches to focus the organisation, staff and young people on asset-based, strength-focused work.

Developed considerably by David Cooperrider, *Appreciative Inquiry* is the search for the best in people, their organisations, and the world around them. Appreciative Inquiry involves searching out what gives 'life' to a living system when it is most alive, and most effective.

The organisational impact of Appreciative Inquiry is to establish a community of people committed to change, enthusiastic about the possibilities of the future, and pledged, in one sense or another, to work for it.

Appreciative Inquiry is a particular approach to asking questions and envisioning the future that fosters positive relationships and builds on the basic assets of a person, a situation, or an organisation. In so doing, it enhances a system's capacity for change and collective working.

Appreciative Inquiry utilises a 4-stage process focusing on:

1. **Discover:** The identification of organisational processes that work well.
2. **Dream:** The envisioning of processes that would work well in the future.
3. **Design:** Planning and prioritising processes that would work well.
4. **Deliver:** The implementation of the proposed design.

The basic idea is to build organisations around what works, rather than trying to fix what doesn't. It is the opposite of problem-solving. The method aims to create meaning by using real success stories.

Well connected, with real partnerships

There is a key parallel between personal and organisational partnerships. Both are formed around a relationship that forms an association between two or more people or groups. This association may be based on emotions like respect or trust, regular business interactions, or some other type of social or work commitment.

Partnership is one of the most used and most misunderstood buzz-words of the last decade. There is no doubt that collaborative and joined up working can have benefits for ourselves and those with whom we work. However, it is important to realise that just because we call something a partnership it doesn't make it a genuine collaboration.

In my mind, partnerships should focus on doing those things that only they can do – and that no-one else and no other grouping can do better or more efficiently. In my experience the key to successful partnership working is two-fold. First, the partners need to be able to work together with mutual understanding and integrity. Secondly, the partnership must have a strong commitment to evaluation and understanding the progress they are making and how they are making it.

Priorities for action

In the last section of the chapter, I identify three aspects of organisational life that could form the focus of action and change. Together, they provide a strong foundation from which to grow continued success.

1. Establish an asset-based philosophy

In their pathway publication on building communities from the inside out Kretzmann and McKnight (1993: 4) explain two different approaches to setting and maintaining a direction of travel for your organisation; needs-driven, and asset-based, internally-focused and relationship-driven.

They say that the two different approaches have these outcomes. Needs-driven organisations:

- View the community as an endless list of problems;
- Can add to a cycle of dependency within communities;
- By their nature find it very difficult to engage the full community.

Asset-based, internally-focused and relationship-driven organisations:

- Focus on the capacities of their communities on what can be achieved and by whom;
- Focus on problem solving and learning from a shared organisational and community perspective, so learning stays in the hand of those who experience it;
- Initiate and grow relationships and trust across communities and organisations mutually.

Genuine and lasting organisation success will only come from an appreciation of local need and working from an asset-based approach.

Instead of focusing on a community's needs, deficiencies and problems, the asset-based approach helps communities become stronger and more self-reliant by discovering, mapping and mobilising their assets. Three key examples of the assets of a community are:

- The skills of its citizens, the young, the old and the in between.
- The dedication of its community associations – churches, interest groups, clubs.
- The resources of its formal institutions – businesses, schools, libraries, colleges, hospitals.

According to the UK Centre for Applied Positive Psychology, an organisation's greatest assets are its people's strengths. But these assets are not always well understood or managed. Everyone has strengths. But not everyone is clear about what their strengths are and how to use them. Critically for organisations, neither are their managers.

Building on strengths

Experience shows that by building on strengths and assets in an organisation can:
(a) *Tap into unused talent throughout the organisation.* There is untapped talent and energy in the organisation. Much time and resource is spent in attempting to improve performance, but little of that is directed at getting the best out of people.
(b) *Attract and retain more of the people it needs.* People like to use their strengths: doing so reinforces and re-energises them. Without the opportunity to use their abilities, many people leave.
(c) *Improve individual performance.* Individual performance is significantly improved by a focus on strengths. The traditional approach of moulding individuals to jobs and focusing on correcting weaknesses has proved unsuccessful.

(d) *Build employee engagement.* Use of strengths is one of the key drivers of employee engagement, which itself is linked to improved employee retention, discretionary effort, quality, customer satisfaction and loyalty.

(e) *Develop flexibility.* Selected and deployed on the basis of strengths – less on the basis of what they 'have done', and more on the basis of what they 'could do' – employees are more willing and able to accept changes in role and organisation.

(f) *Improve teamwork.* A focus on strengths in teams allows for the efficient allocation of tasks and, with greater role flexibility, encourages co-operation. The positive emotions generated by the use of strengths enable social integration.

(g) *Increase diversity and positive inclusion.* An understanding of strengths encourages people to value difference. Teams made up of people who differ tend to be more creative and to perform better.

(h) *Increase openness to change and the ability to deal with change.* The use of strengths generates positive emotions which facilitate performance by broadening people's mindsets.

(i) *Deal more positively with redundancy.* A strengths perspective supports the understanding of redundancy as a mismatch, rather than an absence, of talent.

(j) *Contribute to the happiness and fulfilment of employees.* Apart from being more likely to achieve their goals, people who use their strengths experience higher levels of energy, well-being and authenticity.

2. Build a creative, 'can-do' organisational culture

Organisational culture is an idea in the field management that describes the psychology, attitudes, experiences, beliefs and values – both the personal and cultural values of an organisation.

Schein defines organisational culture as:

> A pattern of basic assumptions, invented discovered, or developed by a given group, as it learns to cope with problems of external adaption and internal integration, that has worked well enough to be considered valid and, therefore, to be taught to new members as the correct way you perceive, think, and feel in relation to those problems. (Quoted in Goodstein, Nolan and Pfeiffer, 1993: 15.)

Schein also asserts that culture is the most difficult organisational attribute to change, outlasting work programmes or services offered to young people, individual, staff and all other physical attributes of the organisation. Modern anthropology distinguishes between internal understandings of cultural events and the understanding of the observer.

In the context of a successful local youth work organisation, it is vital to understand what young people value in the youth work and not just what organisations or funders want them to value or understand. Young people's own terms and experience are the foundation for the formulation of all successful and sustainable youth work programmes.

Doing what you say you'll do

Often described to me as 'the way we do things around here', organisational culture can be as simple or complicated as we choose to make it. Looking back, my own priority has been to concentrate on doing what we say we will do as an organisation. If we say we are going to be there at certain times on certain nights, then we will be there.

In practice, the key phrase has been 'attention to detail'. And that attention has to be paid from the planning stages, not just in 'delivery'. In fact, it is at the planning stages where attention to detail is probably most important. We would give more time collectively to checking that we felt that what we were planning was appropriate to the organisation – and that we were going about our tasks in a way that was compatible with our organisational values.

Over the long-term, consistency and commitment – and consistency of commitment – will establish an organisation as a trusted partner and ally – for young people, for the community and for other organisations. Doing what you say you'll do helps to establish a 'virtuous circle' of increasing success.

Sometimes it can be hard to maintain the 'can-do', optimistic outlook! One vital strategy for maintaining that 'glass half-full' outlook is to surround yourself with other 'can-do' people. One way of sustaining the work is to actively network with other practitioners with a similar outlook (see Chapter 9). The networks can be local, regional national – even international, thanks to the development of the internet. It may mean joining formal networks or it may mean making time to go out for informal chats with colleagues (from the same or different fields) – or going to conferences, logging on to interesting sites and joining various forums. Whatever form it takes, that support of like-minded colleagues is essential succour to potentially isolated practitioners.

3. Create time for reflection

The ability to reflect in and on action is the 'golden thread' that runs through any successful organisation. Reflecting in action are defined by Schön (1983) as the ability of professionals to 'think what they are doing while they are doing it'. He regards this as a key skill.

Schön asserts that the only way to manage the 'indeterminate zones of (professional) practice' is through the ability to think on your feet, and apply previous experience to new situations. This is the essential work of the professional, and requires the capability of reflection-in-action. He asserts that reflecting on action is made after the event, that it is consciously undertaken, and often documented.

Organisations need the ability to think on their feet, adapt to change and record reflections in order to inform future actions. Creating time for reflection is probably the single most important practical action organisations can take to uplift their performance.

Continually taking stock

Giving time for reflection enables individuals and organisations to take stock, to give context to their activities and to clarify exactly what is 'working' and what's not. The reflection can – and should – take place at personal, team and organisational levels:

- Personally: staff members are encouraged to think through their own ideas before bringing them to the team; non-managerial supervision can play a valuable role here.
- As a team: team reflection is especially valuable in the planning stages of projects – a valuable way of 'testing out' practical ideas and of checking that plans match with organisational values.
- Organisationally: structured staff meetings, with prepared agendas, can help organisations to avoid the 'hijacking' of agendas by so-called 'crises'

In the context of Rank's *Youth or Adult?* programme, the emphasis on reflection illustrates the impact and effectiveness of the YMCA George Williams College's approach to learning. The course sets up a way of working that, because of its success, workers and managers give a high priority to incorporating it into their 'regular' practice. Within my own former organisation, involving staff in the College's Diploma Studies reinforced the importance of reflection. And it also helped us to build our own distinctive culture and ethos.

On reflection

Like young people, local organisations are complex, subject to change at a minute's notice and are strongly influenced by the environment in which they exist. Successful local organisations are underpinned and driven by a set of values that, in their most fundamental state, seek association, connection and learning.

In many ways, success relies on a positive state of mind and the ability to look towards (and create) the future. Individuals and organisations looking to raise their levels of success can benefit from a focus on using an asset-based approach, adopting a 'can-do' approach and by taking time to reflect on their activity.

I hope that this chapter has challenged you and inspired you to reflect on your own organisation and has encouraged you to work *on* your organisation as well as *in* it!

Questions for reflection

- What, for you, makes an organisation a 'local' organisation?
- How do you assess the 'connectedness' of your organisation. . .within the local community and beyond?
- How important do you see these organisational characteristics: mindset, envisioning, being resilient and having role models?
- Are any of the organisational characteristics particularly important for your own organisation?
- How could you address the three priorities for action in your own organisation? Is one of them more important than the others for you?
  o Establish an asset-based approach?
  o Build a creative, 'can-do' organisational culture?
  o Create time for reflection?

Growing youth workers in local communities

CHAPTER 4

Finding and recognising youth workers

Judith Skinner

A single word even may be a spark of inextinguishable thought.

Percy Bysshe Shelley

The ability to recognise potential in people is a skill that is seldom explored in youth work literature – but it is essential for the continuation of a thriving and credible profession, as well as for general human flourishing.

This chapter explores some of the ways in which managers, workers and funders can find and recognise potential youth workers. In particular, I examine:

- The 'spark' – that unquantifiable mixture of skills, personality, knowledge and attitudes that represents the potential to work constructively with young people;
- The relationship between professionals and potential youth workers; and
- The ways in which organisational culture and theories of participation enable talent to be nurtured and encouraged.

Beginnings in youth work

How do people get into youth work? Every youth worker – paid or voluntary – has their own story. They may describe how they had never even heard of youth work but suddenly realised, maybe after months or years of involvement, that it was what they were doing. They may talk about how they got into youth work, perhaps through their church or because of their own children, through teaching or their passion for sport, the arts or the environment – or through volunteering, motivated by a desire to help in their local community.

Some people will have attended youth clubs themselves, when they were young, and will have grown through a series of clear stages into youth leadership. But many have had no personal experience of youth work. This experience is typical:

> *I've always enjoyed sport, playing football and basketball at school and with my local club. Anyway, when I left school, I got into the painting and decorating trade, like my dad – it paid the bills, but was just a job as far as I was concerned.*
>
> *I got involved with a football skills coaching course about five years ago and, at the end of the course, began to volunteer at an after-school sports club at my local YMCA. When a part-time job for a Youth Sports Worker at the YMCA was advertised, I jumped at it. I never really knew that people could get paid for informal work with young people! Three years on I'd completed a NVQ in Youth Work and was worker-in-charge of the centre's youth sports programme. Something that I would never had predicted when I left school.*

Often a progression into youth work is not something that individuals plan but, once they are involved in informal education, they find the satisfaction and challenges of the work have an irresistible pull. In addition to the fulfilment derived from enabling others to discover their potential, some youth workers speak of the personal sense of vocation that they receive from their work.

As well as describing the skills and activities that propelled them into youth work, many youth workers mention the presence of key people, who inspired them and enabled them seriously to consider the possibility of becoming a youth worker.

How do these inspirational figures recognise that someone is 'youth worker material'? Do they have a manual that helps them find promising raw talent that they can nurture into a fully-fledged professional? Do they have a 'sixth sense' when it comes to identifying people with the values and attitudes that are essential for good youth workers? Or do they just guess and hope they are encouraging the right person?

Youth work's core values

There are many ways in which we define ourselves or others define us in our occupational identities (Tucker, 2005). The demands of youth work mean that successful workers can come from any background or set of circumstances, but they do need to demonstrate an understanding of certain core values and display appropriate attitudes and awareness based on these.

At the beginning of a youth worker's career, it is likely that they will not have had much opportunity to study the principles and practices of informal education in great depth. They may not have pondered the theories of education or human relationships that underpin the work of professional youth workers. But, hopefully, they will have had plenty of time to experience interacting and building relationships with other people. It is these experiences, coupled with an individual's family background and friendship groups, that provide the opportunity to test out the core values of youth work (Jeffs and Smith, 2005):

- respect for persons
- promotion of well-being
- truth
- democracy
- fairness and equality

These core values can also provide a reference point for workers wishing to identify the 'spark' within others. This is not to suggest that someone will present workers with a clear indication of their potential for youth work; rather that, over time, this will become apparent. It is worth noting that some of the most 'unlikely' young people may go onto develop into excellent youth workers. But how do we spot that potential?

The nature of the 'spark'

Youth workers are as human, diverse and unique as anyone else! As Larry Parsons (2002) argues in his book *Youth Work and the Spark of the Divine*:

> . . . everyone has a divine spark in them – it is my belief that the first aim of every teacher, whether in schools or more informally in the local community . . . should be to discover the spark in each of their charges, to look for the talents we all have in some measure (Parsons, 2002: 7).

When a youth worker starts to consider whether someone has the potential to become an informal educator, they are probably not doing so through an intellectual analysis. Rather, they will instinctively experience that person through their own orientation and this feeling will lead them to reflect on the possibility that there could be an 'informal educator in the making'.

There is no checklist or 'one-size-fits-all' scorecard that could be used to identify the 'spark' of youth worker potential in others. Nevertheless, any youth worker looking for that spark could reflect on the following:

1. **Potential to relate:** the desire to connect with other people is a fundamental skill for youth workers. They must be deeply interested in human relations and posses the ability to build relationships. Other implicit skills in this core of the work include sensitivity to others and the ability to empathise. Whether a person is helpful, disruptive, shy or loud is almost beside the point, as is whether they are always in the centre or on the margins of groups. Whatever their personality, do they demonstrate an interest in and a desire to understand and get on with other people?
2. **Potential to care:** does the person demonstrate altruism towards others and seek to increase their well-being? Do they show empathy and understanding? This does not mean that they continually seek to do things for other people or are 'nice' or a martyr, but they demonstrate an unsentimental and rational desire to do 'good' – something that is rather out of fashion in a society dominated by commercial and consumerist values. In some ways, what we are looking for is a sense of vocation, a calling to relate to and behave towards other people based on a belief of inherent human worth and potential. Or as Parker J. Palmer (1993, xxiv) describes it: 'the spiritual life, the quest for God, which relies on the eye of the heart.' The opportunities may be few and far between. Nevertheless, the ability to care about others is a basic human need. Does the person, regardless of what others think about them, find that they want to treat people well and help them?
3. **Potential to effect change:** youth workers need to be able to reflect on their relationships with young people, fellow workers, agency and community partners and ask what could be done differently. This could relate to the seemingly trivial – reorganising the rota to look after the coffee bar – to the vitally important – taking part in a young person's exclusion meeting at school. Change for change's sake is not a healthy thing. We are not talking about novelty here. It is just as an important skill to recognise what works well and stick to it. However, potential youth workers do need to look at their world with clarity and perspective and ask themselves – does it need to be like this? And, if not, what are the underlying causes of the problems? Does a potential worker demonstrate the desire to

change things for the better in their community, their school and their own life?

4. **Potential for leadership:** youth workers need to be confident in their own abilities and their desire to enable the young people with whom they engage. The word 'leader' in this context does not refer to a dictator who barks orders at other people and expects immediate compliance. A leader is an individual with the strength and confidence to hold other people's well-being as paramount and is committed to doing all they can to nurture it. Youth workers should also have a high regard for the principles of democracy and, as leaders, they should work to ensure that all young people they work with have the same rights and opportunities. Potential leaders will certainly not be the loudest or, necessarily, the most able young people but they will have belief in themselves and a desire to help others achieve what is best for their well-being. Does the potential informal educator demonstrate the ability to make others stop and think? . . . do they participate and encourage? . . . do they want to increase opportunity for others?

5. **Potential to reflect:** the need to think about and process past actions and behaviour is of paramount importance to youth workers. Without this ability, individuals are condemned to repeat mistakes and are unable to gain insight into other people's behaviour – or, indeed, their own. In young people the desire to talk situations through and seek advice can be encouraging signs of reflection. A potential youth worker may also be able to demonstrate the awareness of possibility of change and learning – that they are not condemned to repeat mistakes or always be seen in a particular way. Whatever a young person's behaviour, are they willing to talk about what they have done and use past experience to inform their present understanding and their future actions?

This is not a definitive list – and we are talking about *potential*, rather than established qualities. But, an exploration of the potential to relate, care, change, lead and reflect will highlight some of the key attributes that youth workers should be looking for when 'potential' spotting.

A word of warning, though: keep your eyes and mind open. Human beings, be they potential youth workers or anyone else, can continually surprise us. And remember, as Shelley reminds us in the quotation that opens the chapter – a single word or action can be a clue to budding youth work talent.

'Eyes wide open'

It is an awareness and demonstration of these 'potentials' that youth workers will look for in the informal educators of the future. Nevertheless, when youth workers were asked whether their initial feelings about a potential worker were carefully thought through or a 'gut instinct', they tended to value the latter.

It's a feeling that you just get about some young people – later on you might try to rationalise it. But to start with you just think 'they get it'.

youth work manager

I would say it's a 'heart' rather than a 'head' thing. Some stuff can be taught later but the desire to make a difference can't be learnt in a book. That's what I'm looking for . . .

youth worker

The ability to recognise potential in people strikes at the heart of the 'pain of disconnection' that P.J. Palmer (1993: x) speaks of when referring to the experience of many educators. Palmer highlights the isolation that all of us feel at times when we are tasked to produce results without due reference to our needs as social beings and when 'hope, optimism and social commitment are not in abundance' (Halpin, 2003). At such times the youth worker requires a subtle mix of knowledge, skills and attitude, as well an innate ability to get alongside other people and begin to know them.

The more experienced worker needs an understanding of what makes a 'good' youth worker – some adherence to the core values listed above and the ability to translate them into practical action would be a good place to start. Through their informal education practice – building relationships, communication, empathy and self-awareness – the worker will get to know the potential trainee and begin to foster their learning and development.

Perhaps most importantly, the worker needs to have their eyes and ears open to the possibility of potential in the people with whom they engage. It could be argued that this should go without saying. However, in an increasingly bureaucratic and funding-led environment, having time to build relationships with young people and responding in a creative and spontaneous way to them has become a precious commodity.

The experienced worker also has to posses the honesty, generosity and good sense to work with everyone in a way that encourages their potential to blossom. Workers need a good degree of self-awareness to respond effectively to different people and not simply to promote those who say what they want to hear, flatter them or fulfil the image of a potential trainee youth worker. This requires workers to be open to each individual and hold their talents, aspirations and needs as unique.

The ability to identify and nurture the 'spark' is a complex mixture of quantifiable and unquantifiable factors and awareness of the individual's developmental progression. Youth workers need time to reflect on people's substance – their fundamental qualities – rather than their superficial appearance. A lot of this process is trial and error – a combination of giving young people opportunities to take greater responsibility and observing how they respond to it. Nevertheless, despite all the planning, development opportunities and self-awareness available to experienced youth workers, there also appears to a fair degree of luck involved in fostering the potential of a particular young person.

A wide range of factors and issues, from the personal to the organisational, can derail the process at any stage. Many workers speak of a serendipitous element in this aspect of youth work. Unlooked-for potential – and the opportunities to nurture it – can be unplanned, can involve the most unlikely people, and yet be full of learning and revelation for all of those who participate in the process of self-discovery.

Opportunities for nurturing the 'spark'

Workers must listen carefully to people's hopes for the future and compare this to their behaviour and the way they treat others. There must then be the opportunity to take greater responsibility within the youth project.

Opportunities for youth workers to support and encourage young people's developmental journey can be thin on the ground in the current climate:

> *Everything has to be planned so far in advance these days. If we want to take young people off-site, we have to complete a form and get agreement two weeks in advance. I seem to spend more and more time filling in record sheets about predicted and achieved outcomes and applying for funding, than talking to young people. You really have to be determined to spend time with young people and be responsive to them – it's so easy to get pulled in other directions . . .*
>
> senior youth worker

The aims and the environment of the individual agency will have a major effect on a worker's ability to find and recognise potential. Some organisations will see a young leaders programme or trainee worker scheme as central to their mission, for others it will be more of a sideline or non-existent.

The ability to recognise and encourage development is largely dependent on the skills and attitudes of the youth worker, coupled with the determination shown by the young person, rather than the presence of any programme. Yet, without the supportive culture of their agency and the opportunities presented by a specific programme, the translation of potential into practical skills and knowledge can be limited.

There are currently a number of full-time placement-based 'gap' schemes, including those run by the Prince's Trust and the youth organisation, and Community Service Volunteers (CSV). Many other third sector agencies have run their own full-time volunteer programmes for older young people. However, these schemes do not purport to provide opportunities for trainee youth workers and, for many young people, the focus of their placement is not youth work, but a host of other community-driven objectives.

Similarly, some statutory youth services provide development opportunities for young people through their own in-house schemes, the nationally recognised Youth Achievement Awards or the well-known Duke of Edinburgh Award. Others offer progression through a variety of youth participation programmes, such as the Participation Works scheme, supported by the National Youth Agency and other voluntary national youth organisations.

Rather than describing the mechanics of how different programmes work, it is probably of greater use in this context to dwell on the common features that they all provide for youth work to maximise opportunities to support progression into informal education. The common features of the programmes mentioned above include the opportunity for:

- Self development and discovery.
- Revealing potential.
- Confidence building.
- Work in people and relationship building.
- Increasing self-awareness.
- Innovative approaches to learning.
- Achievement and celebration.

These features are the glue that holds any young leaders' or achievement programme together, regardless of the mechanics of a particular scheme or the hoops that a young person has to jump through to make progress.

The Rank Gap Scheme

The Rank Foundation's Gap Scheme offers an opportunity for both working and learning within informal education.

Perhaps one of the common characteristics of agencies funded by the Rank Foundation is that they aspire to or already have a young leaders' development scheme.

The Foundation has always paid close attention to the massive potential for individual development and organisational enhancement that the training and support of new youth workers can bring. Its Gap Scheme is a recognised leader in its field, providing support and guidance for agencies that want to enable older young people to make the transition into youth workers.

The Scheme has been in existence since 1992 and was initially developed to provide young people, who had been supported by the Rank Foundation at school, the opportunity to work at a grassroots level with a community-based agency.

Latterly, the Rank Gap Scheme, as it became known, has provided more opportunities for young people within the youth agencies that receive financial support from the Foundation. As such, it has made a major contribution to facilitating young leader development.

All young people participating in the Rank Gap Scheme have the opportunity to study a VRQ level 3 in Diploma Studies in Informal Education at the YMCA George Williams College. Their placements are well supported, both financially and practically, by the joint endeavours of their 'home' agency and the Rank Foundation.

The Scheme provides an excellent way of facilitating young people's development and providing them with the opportunity to find out whether youth and community work is for them.

For more details see Rogers (2005) and Rank Foundation (2009b)

On the same journey

From the point of view of the young person whose 'spark' is spotted, the involvement of the worker is a powerful influence. But the influence is two-way – youth workers encourage young people on the first steps of a developmental journey – a journey they are still making themselves.

The most experienced and knowledgeable informal educator was a young person themselves once! Although they may have years of line management, report and grant writing, teaching and curriculum design, everybody had to start somewhere in their youth work journey. For some, the journey and the distance travelled will have been truly phenomenal, for others it will appear to have been straightforward. Nevertheless, all will have gained insight and self-knowledge.

Journeying together

Stories from the Rank Foundation network illustrate the two-way process of 'journeying together', as worker and young person – and then as worker and trainee.

Over the past 22 years the Rank Foundation has worked with hundreds of young people and youth workers in community-based agencies to develop potential and foster growth.

The core *Youth or Adult?* programme has always focused on the support and professional development of an individual (Rogers and Smith, 2008). During this time there have been some amazing journeys, with accompanying stories from those that have participated in Rank's programmes.

The stories range from the inspiring:

> *It has allowed me to learn so much about me – my own purpose in life and that's a great experience – there's nothing like knowing who you are . . .*
>
> youth support worker

To the down to earth and realistic:

> *I come from the same community as these young people and because they've seen me around they allow me to sit with them . . . They need to find a way to better themselves and through experience they find that better way . . . we just need to be with them really.*
>
> trainee youth worker

Other workers focus on the cyclical nature of learning and the sense of progression that they experience, while enabling young people:

> *You learning about you, while learning about other people . . .*
>
> youth worker

And – as a recognition of the two-way benefits:

> *I play a part in their support and their continued journey. It's amazing!*
>
> youth work manager

I remember my delight and terror when I was asked by my senior worker to lead a session at the Youth Arts Centre, where I was on placement at the age of 22. I also recall the moment, about six months later, when, thanks to a chance comment from another worker, all those seemingly meaningless chats and games of pool I'd been having suddenly made sense! I realised that simply being there with young people, getting to know and understand them was the essential starting point for devising opportunities to increase their learning and development . . . now I just had to work out how I was going to take those next steps!

In many ways, the challenge for a professional youth worker is to hang on to the enthusiasm and idealism that often comes easily to young people and place it within a framework of experience and knowledge.

The majority of youth workers will remember with feeling the initial spark that inspired them to become informal educators. I hope all youth workers continue to remember those first steps and hang on to some of the thoughts and feelings that accompanied their early days in youth and community work.

Perhaps the overriding message is that it is the ability to reflect, learn and change themselves that makes it possible for youth workers to find, recognise and nurture other potential informal educators.

Reflections

This chapter has explored the challenges and opportunities inherent in finding and recognising potential youth workers. It has examined the nature of the 'spark' that some people possess – the unquantifiable mixture of attitude, skills and knowledge that makes an informal educator.

For a person's potential as a youth worker – or as anything else for that matter – to be unleashed, it has first to be recognised by someone else. Youth workers need to stay awake to the potential of the people with whom they engage and have great aspirations for them.

Youth workers also need to maintain their own sense of self-belief and their capacity to be responsive to people around them. They are key motivators for young people on their journey of self-discovery. But workers also need to acknowledge that those young people may play a significant part in *their* journey, too.

Questions for reflection

- How does your own introduction to work with young people impact on your approach to work now?
- Are there any young people you have a feeling might be potential youth workers? . . . how did that feeling grow?
- How can you help increase potential in any of the five areas of 'spark' identified? . . . are there any priorities among them?
- Are there other 'potentialities' you might look for in young people who could make good youth work practitioners?
- Where do you see your own greatest potential? . . . and the area that you would most like to develop?

CHAPTER 5

Developing committed and informed workers

Jeff Salter

The qualities that show a person's 'spark' of potential as an informal educator will need to be nurtured, in order to maintain their personal and professional energy.

The first part of this chapter examines the goal of becoming a 'committed and informed' worker. I then explore how workers, managers and organisations can create the conditions to enable this kind of personal and professional development. While acknowledging the pressures that work against it, I offer managers a template for encouraging growth – by 'believing in', 'bringing out' and 'building around' their workers.

Being 'committed and informed'

Workers who maintain their initial enthusiasm and excitement for the work – their 'spark' – several years down the line, are genuine change-makers. They are resilient, resourceful and calm in the face of difficulties; they encourage young people, team members and managers to 'journey together'. They are researchers and learners – they reflect on their own practice and gain valuable lessons from others. People like and respect them. I have chosen to encapsulate these qualities by naming them 'committed and informed'.

In attempting to define the concept of a committed and informed worker, both workers and managers point towards a common factor – that of the 'integrity' or 'state of mind' of the individual. There seems to be a value-based, attitudinal core to the 'committed and informed' worker, regardless of personality type or work situation.

Stephen Covey describes the characteristics of the 'principled-centred leader'. He suggests that 'these traits not only characterise effective leaders, they also serve as signs of progress for all of us' (1999: 33). We might, therefore, consider if these principles underscore the approach of workers *and* of the managers who are keen to support them:

1. They are continually learning

Covey states that principle-centred people 'read, seek training, take classes, listen to others . . . they are curious, always asking questions. They continually expand their competence, their ability to do things' (1999: 33). As informal educators of principle, we are driven to seek knowledge, especially about the connection between ourselves and others. We challenge and theorise about our work and the human condition, and we want to learn more about who we are and the 'why' and 'how' of the work we do. One worker describes this as 'the willingness to be open to learning, whether trained or not'.

The path for many workers is through professional qualification, yet at a fundamental level, an acceptance that learning can come from any source, particularly the young people and communities with whom we work, encapsulates this particular principle.

However, we need to be discerning about this learning – not indiscriminate 'sponges' of material, but making considered reflections on that learning, regardless of the source. An openness to continual learning is, therefore, supported by the growing ability to reflect on that learning. Do workers accept supervision, for example, as instruction on or verification of their practice? . . . or are they developing the confidence and knowledge to use it as a tool for exploration and change?

2. They are service-oriented

Covey's view is that 'life is a mission not a career' (1999: 34). We might, therefore, consider to what extent we are committed to the work we do. Doyle and Smith describe the act of service: '(it) involves doing tasks for the benefit of others. For us, it is an act of heart. It is undertaken in the spirit of the community, of being part of, and connected with a larger whole' (1999: 42). This suggests both a desire to work for the benefit of others *and* to join in a sense of community with those we are serving.

Whether or not workers live in the area they work – and whether or not they have difficulties with the organisation in which they work – we must ask the question: do they have an overall feel for the community in which they are located and the community of practice of which they are part? Covey speaks of the need to 'pull together' with the people with whom we are working, for the sake of the community we are serving. This must override our personal and professional differences. We need regularly to question ourselves about our motives and priorities.

Covey (1999: 34) speaks of the responsibility, the 'yoke', even, of this service:

> In effect, every morning, they 'yoke up' and put on the harness of service, thinking of others ... I have come to believe that effort to become principle-centred without a load to carry simply will not succeed ... if we do not have a sense of responsibility, of service, of contribution, something we need to pull or push, it becomes a futile endeavour.

I would prefer to see this responsibility as a privilege rather than a burden. The responsibility to care for others is often seen this way. Serving a community with whom we have built a relationship based on trust over time is seen as a gift, and this attitude marks out many successful projects and individuals. As one worker says: *'this is what I do and I love it!'*

3. They radiate positive energy

Covey (1999: 34) says the following of such leaders: 'their attitude is optimistic, positive, upbeat. Their spirit is enthusiastic, hopeful, believing'. There are many dilemmas and issues facing youth work today. Uncertain funding, increasing pressures and demanding targets have changed the face of the field at lightning pace. Sometimes these pressures feel overbearing – yet we are drawn to those who can confront such difficulties with optimism and good humour. These individuals are often characterised by their resilience in the face of difficulty, are aware of their own needs for support and care at certain times, yet act as a beacon to others through this energy.

4. They believe in other people

Covey states that principle-centred leaders 'don't over-react to negative behaviours, criticism or human weaknesses. They are not naïve ... but they realise that behaviour and potential are two different things' (1999: 35). Informed and committed workers need to not only discern the difference between behaviour and potential in young people, but also extend that insight to the teams they work in, the people they manage, and the people who manage them. The most effective leaders are, as one worker put it: *'like the stabilisers for my bike'*.

They know to encourage learning through challenge, rather than inhibiting it through criticism. They recognise that mistakes are important for growth. They work 'alongside' others rather than 'over' or 'above' them; and they have a desire to know about others and what makes them tick (and not only when it is advantageous and convenient for them to do so). They also know when to take away the stabilisers and let workers wobble away on their own bikes!

In summary, being 'informed and committed' means that workers are:

- Open to learning from all directions and can discern which elements of this learning are of value.
- Regard being able to serve their communities and their peers as a gift.
- Encourage and excite people with their zest and spirit for what they do especially in adversity.
- Believe in others to the extent of working alongside them rather than over them.

These attributes are not created in a vacuum. To a certain extent, of course, workers will need to possess personal qualities in these areas – the 'spark'. But what conditions need to be present within organisations for these qualities to flourish? How might managers encourage and support workers to make the most of their potential? What can managers do to encourage an environment of commitment to the work, a desire to develop effective working relationships and value a culture of learning?

The challenge for managers

The goal of creating a climate for personal and professional growth provides a major challenge for managers. Not only do they themselves require the qualities of a 'committed and informed' worker, they have a responsibility to nurture those qualities in the staff they manage.

Lee Bolman and Terrence Deal, writing for a broader readership, echo many statements made within our field about what constitutes effective management:

> . . . we need managers who love their work and their organisations and the people whose lives they affect. We need leaders and managers who appreciate management as a moral and ethical undertaking. We need leaders who combine hard-headed realism with passionate commitment to larger values and purposes (2008: viii).

It is not easy for managers in informal education today to provide this template for workers, yet workers have never needed it more. When workers were asked what elements of organisational life contributed to their motivation and commitment, it was easier for some to reflect on their organisation's shortcomings, those elements that caused them to lack motivation and commitment. Areas of concern included:

- favouritism
- power struggles
- poor listening skills
- unwillingness to compromise
- not flexible enough/too flexible
- 'target obsessed'
- lack of tolerance
- lack of transparency
- laziness masquerading as delegation

These responses suggest that fear, lack of time and other external pressures, as well as elements of control, power, and interpersonal skills, can impact detrimentally on workers' development.

It is easy to understand why it might be difficult to respond creatively in some of the high-pressure circumstances prevalent in the field today. The pace of change in both statutory and voluntary sectors continues at a rate undreamed of a few years ago. Workers are confused and seek understanding and guidance. Managers are distracted, 'fire-fighting', living on their wits and lose the impetus to work creatively and inclusively with their staff.

Yet the commitment and loyalty of workers often depends on managers who have the time, energy and will to embrace the complexity of managing their staff teams. When under pressure, managers can get stuck in repetitive and unproductive responses to their staff teams needs. '*I know he's under pressure, but the constant criticism is getting me down*' observed one worker.

Bolman and Deal suggest that 'managers who master the hammer and expect all problems to behave like nails will find life at work confusing and frustrating' (2008: 13). Workers who are 'hammered' by their managers are not only 'flattened' in the here-and-now, but learn lessons for their future in how to respond to pressures in similarly one-dimensional ways.

The challenge is to blend 'clarity with creativity' (Bolman and Deal, 2008: 74). Targets need to be met; the quality of an organisation's work is often measured by its ability to deliver outcomes on time, on budget and to a high standard. To do this ensures future funding, inspires confidence in both staff and the communities they serve. Yet managers who want their workers to commit to and be informed about the work they do, will go beyond the bottom line.

Believing in, bringing out, building around

When questioned about support from managers, workers were clear that they appreciated managers who expressed and showed their commitment to *them* as well as a commitment to the aims of the organisation, that the culture of the organisation, the 'way of doing things', mirrored the overt messages about what the organisation stood for to the community it served. In other words: is the mission statement truly reflected within organisational life, as well as in the annual report?

Workers value managers who are interested in them as people, as well as workers. Plas and Lewis (2001: 161) reflect on this same issue:

> A person-centred approach is different from other sorts of participatory and empowerment approaches. Yes, employees participate, and yes, they are empowered. But in addition, employees receive the message that their personal and professional development is just as important as the organisation's mission. In fact, the organisation is construed to have a dual mission: the development of the individual employee and the stated product or service goal.

This approach can be split into three distinct components:

- **Believing in** – whether workers are 'going it alone' or 'under the wing', workers want appreciation and recognition for what they do *and* who they are.
- **Bringing out** – this can best be expressed as the insight and confidence managers need to enable workers to grow.
- **Building around** – workers need both management systems and emotional support, in order to maintain and sustain their growth and development.

Let's look at these three areas in more detail, and identify what workers and managers have expressed about each of them.

Believing in

'Believing in' is the only starting point for effective staff development. It extends beyond acknowledging and exploring a worker's professional potential. It is about providing an overall environment that allows *them* to do so. That environment requires workers to be appreciated and recognised, not only for the work that they do, but equally for who they are. Workers need to feel significant . . . and feeling significant leads to commitment. As one worker expressed it:

> . . . *people saw potential in me as an individual that I didn't see. They gave me a chance and I'm loyal to that.*

When workers were asked how managers and organisations can build a worker's commitment, some of the replies were that they should demonstrate that they:

- Value the development of the worker and the person.
- Respect skills and the person.
- Recognise what the worker is interested in – and encourage them to pursue it.
- Demonstrate reciprocal commitment.

Managers and organisations must *earn* commitment, rather than anticipate it – much like an effective informal educator. When we are valued for who we are, our beliefs and personalities, we grow in self-belief, and become more resilient in the face of difficult circumstances. When our troubles and concerns are taken seriously, when managers respond compassionately towards us, we are much more likely to re-double our efforts when the going gets tough. As one worker reported about their manager:

> *He didn't agree with my work plan, but he must believe in me, because he supported me with other people – that really encouraged me.*

Edward Hallowell, cited in Peter Frost's *Toxic Emotions at Work*, speaks of the 'human moment' – the key moment when a manager first responds to a worker who comes to them in distress. 'The human moment has two pre-requisites' he writes, 'people's physical presence and their emotional and intellectual attention'. He states that believing in people does not need to be particularly draining or time-consuming:

> To make it work, you have to set aside what you are doing, put down the memo you were reading, disengage from your lap-top, abandon your day dream and focus on the people you are with (Hallowell in Frost, 2007: 22).

We are often overrun with commitments; we may be physically 'there' for our workers, but not present emotionally or intellectually. Putting aside our agendas and being there 'in the moment' for workers may be challenging in the short term, but reaps benefits over time.

'Believing in' is, of course, about professional development; building a worker's skills, so they can be trusted to deliver – and the 'stabilisers' removed. Yet it is also about personal growth. Managers who believe in their workers are likely to be compassionate. They not only encourage their workers' professional endeavours but, according to Frost (2007: 24) they are able to:

> . . . read emotional cues (their own and others) and anticipate their effects in work situations and empathise with those who are hurt and listen to them with care.

Managers with belief model their behaviour as the organisation's cultural norm. It is usual for members of the organisation to care for each other, believe in each other's competence and commitment, rather than suspect each other of incompetence or wrongdoing. From a basis of 'believing in', everything becomes possible.

Bringing out

Passionate and committed managers will invariably have clear ideas about what the organisation should be doing. It is their job to think strategically about the direction the organisation is travelling. Yet, in order to encourage others in the organisation to be passionate and committed to their work, they need to find insight and confidence to know how to 'hold back' and encourage workers by 'bringing out' their abilities.

This involves the creation of an environment that welcomes learning and reflection, rather than certainty. This is often apparent in how an organisation reacts to both people and ideas from outside that organisation. Are we outward or inward looking in our approach towards other agencies and disciplines? What sort of welcome do we give to newcomers to our environment? Does the organisation think about and absorb the ideas from outside, in order to improve?

A manager who 'brings out' their staff will recognise the impact of other people and ideas on a worker's practice as opportunities to be considered, rather than threats to be shunned. One worker expressed how her line manager encouraged her to build on her skills by embracing learning from outside the organisation:

She always says to me, 'do you want to have a try at that?' She puts me forward for things and builds me up. She encouraged me to attend a working with homeless people course that I thought I wouldn't be able to grasp. But she could see I could, and I didn't regret it.

Such managers are also likely to challenge their workers to make decisions in everyday organisational life, and don't purely delegate decision-making when it is beneficial to them to do so. Workers in such a learning environment are, therefore, encouraged to learn from their mistakes rather than be frightened of making them. They are 'informed' by the world of practice around them.

Workers reiterate that they feel important, significant within the organisation, as a result of this approach. In dealings with their managers, they recognise the skill involved in balancing challenge with nurture. The focus of line management sessions, for example, moves from ticking boxes to trying new things. When workers feel significant, their potential is uncovered; encouraged by an insightful manager, they tend not to forget the experience and are changed by it. One experienced manager remembers her introduction to youth work through such insight:

A worker spotted my hidden and not obvious leadership qualities, and that has stayed with me and boosted me.

So, do we provide enough opportunities for leadership to emerge? In working with young people, we often spot transferable strengths . . . do we afford the same opportunities to our staff?

There is no little finesse involved in transmitting one's passion and commitment lucidly and engagingly to others. Bolman and Deal (1991: 11) refer to leaders who can 'bring their audience along. They must use their artistry to articulate and communicate their visions so that others are also able to see things differently'.

Workers commit to organisations where managers hone the ability to include and welcome alternative views and visions, as well as being able to communicate their own. As one worker put it:

My manager has drive, passion, and ideas. But she even thinks of ideas that she can't do, and asks if we can!

The challenge for managers, therefore, is both to lead and to enable. They must aim to provide the stabilisers for the bike when they are needed . . . and time their removal when they are not.

Building around

One worker spoke admiringly of her manager:

She's stable and challenging, nurtures but wants us to get on with it. I got a shock when she asked me to back up my claims with evidence, but it keeps me on my toes, and I know she will support me when I need it.

This worker has identified the necessity to 'build around' staff, in order to provide them with the springboard necessary to achieve their potential. This springboard has two forms:

- Effective systems and structures to establish a fair and well organised working environment.
- Emotional support, including the ability to motivate and empathise with staff, thus building a healthy and happy working environment.

Bolman and Deal speak of the different 'frames' managers need to develop in 'building around' workers. They note the importance of 'structural' and 'human resource' frames, and how managers must strive to incorporate both in their repertoire.

Paradoxically, the 'frames' identified by Bolman and Deal are rooted in conflicting understandings of organisational life. From the 'structural' perspective, staff become de-motivated and interpersonal issues arise when organisational structures are not put in place to manage the origins of these conflicts or difficulties. From this standpoint, a common pattern is where, say, a lack of formal supervision and appraisal lead to staff being demotivated and lacking drive. Get the structures right and the people will follow, seems to be the message.

Conversely, from the 'human resource' perspective, the focus of organisational life is the interplay between individuals or groups. Unless individual needs are met, organisational structures will be circumvented. Indeed, individuals can use structures to hide their difficulties and conflicts, thus avoiding dealing with the personal issue and projecting it as an organisational failure. It is tempting to scapegoat an inanimate system (and implicate someone else) rather than address a live interpersonal conflict, which requires you to recognise your responsibility in finding a solution.

The concept of 'building around', therefore, asks managers to balance these two frames. When questioned about what managers might do to support their practice, workers came up with a range of suggestions that echoes the need for both effective systems *and* emotional support:

- Invest in people for more than a year – this removes unnecessary stress.
- Once/twice a year training (with lunch!).
- Regular one-to-one supervision.
- Personal performance review.
- Socialising outside work.
- Providing a healthy and happy environment.
- Sustainability equals loyalty.

So, how do systems and structures support managers in their development role? Workers regularly spoke of 'stand out' moments in their workplace, times when the actions of their managers have transformed their attitudes:

> At first, it seemed like my manager was just shifting work onto me, but now I see the value. From the start, he had his mind set on me being a co-ordinator, and he was training me up without me even knowing it! . . . Now I am the project co-ordinator, and I work with others in the same way. He didn't just send me on a training course, he encouraged my ideas for training others.
> From day one, my views mattered when I met with my line manager.

These moments are likely to provide workers with a successful template on which to base their own practice.

What is 'support' – and what is so vital about it? Providing a 'healthy and happy working environment' is a big ask and of course, there has to be a team as well as an individual will to create this. However, the suggestion conveyed by both workers and managers is that managers, at least to some extent, need to take responsibility for creating a thriving environment that mirrors the value of mutual respect for each individual. How might managers work towards this?

Brooks and Goldstein (2001: 106) write persuasively about how parents might create a thriving environment for their children. The concepts suggested here seem very transferable to the management role in the context we have been exploring. They talk about the difference between 'builders' and 'chippers':

> A beautiful statue can be created by either starting with a large piece of marble and chipping away or starting with a small lump of clay and building up. Although in the art world either method may produce a beautiful work, in the parenting world, the chipping method is unproductive. Some parents report their frustration after having exerted 'so much energy' in raising their children. Unfortunately, the majority of their energy is directed at chipping away, attempting to shape the child into something

they perceive as desirable. Instead, we advocate the building model; building up rather than chipping down.

In workers' eyes, there seems to be a thin dividing line between 'building' and 'chipping'. There are often cries of lack of support, swiftly followed by equally loud accusations of micro-management! Managers need, perhaps, to discern between offering appreciation, rather than approval, encouragement rather than protection. As one worker stresses:

It feels good to work here because my manager says to me: 'You can do it.' He gives me the opportunity to walk or fall, but at least he allows me to be myself. He checks in on me, says 'yeah, that's good', but he's not patronising. I really value the non-interference.

Building around' is not simply about 'giving' support; it also proposes that the recipient must have a say in what that support might be and whether its delivery is helpful to their development. This can be a difficult and frustrating balance for managers to negotiate. Brooks and Goldstein (2001: 106) suggest that parents (and, I suggest, managers too):

. . . engage with this chipping process without realising it. We pronounce what our children are doing wrong rather than what they are doing right. We correct rather than teach.

Some managers have reported the 'ingratitude' shown to them by the workers for the opportunities, chances and direction 'given' to them. But, as we have seen, workers appear to commit to organisations for different reasons. They see 'support' as 'hands-off' at certain times, as well as the more traditional forms. Although their motives might be admirable, managers may need to consider the extent to which they are 'chippers', eroding the commitment of their workers.

Organisational responsibilities

Ultimately, the challenge to 'build around' a workforce is an organisational one, and we will now examine how organisations might blend 'effective systems and structures' with 'support' for workers as identified above.

First, an easily understood and well-communicated policy around recruitment, induction, supervision, appraisal and training is essential. Workers appreciate it when organisations demonstrate, by their actions, that they care for, support, encourage and set boundaries for them from 'the cradle to the grave', from when they arrive in the organisation to when they leave.

'Living' staff development methods, based on the principles that we, as informal educators, say we believe in, give the message that:

- This is an organisation worth belonging to.
- The organisation is committed to including you and your ideas within it.

This organisational 'building around' the staff encourages commitment even in difficult times. Ongoing financial uncertainty has an effect on workers' morale and confidence. It may not always be possible, especially when organisations suddenly lose funding, to 'build around' workers financially, yet instability can erode the commitment of the most willing workers.

Establishing supportive structures and inclusive methods will encourage workers to be interested in, informed about and, thus able to contribute to the process of finding solutions to the difficult situations that organisations find themselves in, rather than spectating from the sidelines. Are workers able to influence the 'big picture' in organisational life, or is such growth thwarted through fear, secrecy and hierarchy?

To create inclusive working environments, critical choices need to be made about all aspects of staff development, but most significantly:

- How workers are supervised.
- How workers are trained.

We have already discussed the difference between workers being 'instructed through' or 'challenged by' supervision. Organisations that accept and adopt the notion of inclusion within their staff development structures will expect the input of workers to the process of line management. Are workers encouraged to set the agenda for their line management meetings and set and meet their own targets (which are often far more challenging than targets set for them by a third party)? Is there a vital, interactive relationship between the manager and the managed?

Beyond line management supervision, organisations might also consider whether possibilities exist for non-managerial supervision of workers. An organisation committed to learning and reflection, rather than certainty, and which values personal and emotional support for its workers will want to consider offering supervision for their workers away from the line-management function. Here, individuals are able to reflect on their practice with an alternative professional, unattached to the processes, products and politics of the organisation, but with the ability and experience to challenge and probe a worker's thinking.

It is informative to listen to current students of informal education, who have been through an extensive and continuous programme of non-managerial supervision. They are appreciative of the opportunity; they counter the charge that it might be divisive or cause tension with their line managers; and they state that they develop an increased understanding of the values that underpin their work. This clearly has personal and professional benefits, as one student reflected:

> . . . after four years of (non-managerial) supervision, and reflecting on self, I'm no longer afraid of what I don't know.

When considering training for staff, does the training provider reflect the essence of 'continual learning' that Covey speaks of? Does it 'build' up rather than 'chip' away at the student? The principles and approach matter, just as much as the content.

If any training programme, whether a short course or qualifying degree, is to 'build around' workers as students, it must not only recognise the value of experience but also the value of reflecting on that experience. It is not simply the 'doing' but what you think about what you've done that is the catalyst for change.

Training must not only disseminate useful knowledge but should also recognise and encourage recognition of the limitations of that knowledge. It should encourage the notion that the learning experience is a two-way exchange, between the educator and the educated, just as line management recognises this between the manager and the managed. There should also be some ambiguity between who fulfils each of those roles at any one time!

These statements about how external training might reflect the values of the organisation point to questions about the composition and philosophy of that training. With this in mind, organisations might want to consider the following questions when considering training that 'builds around' workers:

- Can trainees understand and build on the impact they have on others, and the impact others have on them?
- Are they challenged to understand what drives them, what 'presses their buttons', how they behave under pressure and how they review and adapt their practice in the light of these understandings?
- Are they encouraged to practice equal opportunities as a state of mind rather than an expression of their 'best behaviour'?
- Are they encouraged to value yet be able to critique the views of others, be it Paulo Freire or a local voluntary worker?

- Are they supported, yet challenged, in their academic endeavours ... encouraged but not smothered, and guided to manage the balance of work, study and life?
- Lastly, are they encouraged to take responsibility for their learning – in a way that lends them integrity and credibility when they encourage young people to do likewise?

Looking to the future

Developing an informed and committed workforce offers big challenges for the field.

In terms of the responsibilities of the workers, we must revisit our underlying motives for working in the field we do, and make an honest examination of our values and attitudes. Do we see the work we do as a privilege? Do we educate with excitement and zest for the challenges we face?

Managers have to look at themselves and their organisations and ask if they are ready to face the external and internal challenges provided by managing informal education in the 21st century creatively and with zest.

As well as providing structures and systems to support them, and opportunities for leadership to emerge, managers have to show, through word and deed, that they trust, value and encourage their workers in their endeavours, both personally and professionally.

These challenges present issues for some organisations that go beyond the realms of this chapter. Where negative behaviours, poor attitudes, creaking systems, and intolerable external pressures have worn down organisations, change may not be possible, at least in the short-term.

Workers and managers have to make their own decisions about what they want and what they are prepared to do within the various contexts in which they find themselves. If they commit to changing their own and their organisation's practice, it is more likely to be a 'slow burn' than a meteoric transformation.

Even when change starts to show, being committed may not result in thanks; much like youth work itself, recognition for our efforts may have to wait. Brooks and Goldstein point out how parents rarely receive thanks for the efforts they make in raising children (2001: 70). In a similar vein, it is rare that workers spend much time being thankful for the wonderful working conditions created for them by their managers!

Nevertheless, the signs from the field are encouraging. Despite prevailing national and local difficulties, workers are reporting some excellent managerial practice and managers are extolling the virtues of their staff. Informed and committed workers abound!

Questions for reflection

- Looking at workers in your agency – beginning with yourself – do you see indicators of 'principle-centred leadership': continual learning; service orientation; positive energy; belief in others? What are those indicators and how can they be built upon?
- In your organisation, how do managers demonstrate that they 'believe in' you and other team members? Where do you see the strengths and areas for development?
- In your organisation, how do managers 'bring out' the confidence and skills of yourself and other team members? Where do you see the strengths and areas for development?
- Do you sense that your organisation has built an appropriate balance of systems and personal and professional support around the staff team? Where do you see the strengths and areas for development?

CHAPTER 6

Strength through struggle

Gemma McDonald

In 2000 I embarked on a course of academic study not fully knowing what to expect or how it would change my life. Although I knew it was about youth work and that it would help develop and challenge me, I had not anticipated the level and depth of change it would generate. Almost like going on a mystery holiday tour I knew my mode of travel and standards of accommodation. My journey was via distance learning (mode of travel) and my standard of accommodation could be a degree in informal education (a bit like having a guaranteed accommodation rating). I would be an independent traveller but would be accompanied on 'tours' with like-minded people who had also embarked on the mystery tour.

Through my story – and the reflections of my fellow student/workers – this chapter demonstrates, identifies and provides examples of the strength gained, the rewards and satisfaction of working through a range of struggles and challenges that youth workers face as part of their journey. I hope you will be able to appreciate and benefit from the experiences of others who have the same passion and motivations to helping others learn.

In 2007 I completed my degree in informal and community education. Now I am managing my own project, developing a consortium approach to youth work in small villages. Following the five-year adventure through the *Youth or Adult?* programme I have grown as a person, and increased in confidence and ability as an informal and community educator. You might at this point be thinking, 'That's all right for her, things are easy now! She has passed; all the stress and struggle are over'. Yeah right! Life is a continuing journey, there will always be challenges, and highs and lows. I enjoy my work, having a stack of responsibilities including managing staff, face-to-face work with young people and facilitating the ongoing politics that is community development. Each day I use what I have experienced and learned to shape the future of my work to guide me in the choices I make.

Life and change can be a personal struggle; striving to be a youth worker can magnify that struggle. But we all know the feeling of satisfaction when achieving something we set out to do. And there can be a greater feeling of satisfaction, when we have to overcome challenges to reach our goal. Success is that much sweeter when we have to sweat for it!

The necessary struggle

Having always been one of those people who joined in and helped – I recognised that working with young people was what made me tick, and that choosing to progress and train as a youth worker would bring challenges and rewards.

When I began my journey I was excited about my potential 'destination', but naïve and unaware of the dark streets and dead ends I would have to take to get there. During the course of my academic study (journey) I was thrust into new experiences: standing up for what I believed in with peer groups, colleagues, parents, friends and young people, made me at times shout and scream, bite my tongue, talk for endless hours, over-examine situations and scenarios, laugh till my sides ached, jump for joy, and cry like a child. All of these things helped make me who I am today.

In being proud of the progress I have made, and what I have achieved, I recognise there were significant periods of 'struggle'. Some things did not come easily, primarily with my study and secondarily around my own self-belief. In addition to a range of learning experiences about line management, time management, and knowing and understanding my role and responsibilities, I knew better who I was and who I was supposed to be.

Self-awareness and self-belief are of fundamental importance. So much of what we do as local workers and informal educators is bound up with who we are and how people experience us. For people to turn to us for help, we have to be experienced as approachable, wise and ready to engage with them. In other words, youth work and community work is:

> . . . heavily dependent on the personality, commitment and knowledge of the worker. So much depends on their relationships with young people, local people, other workers etc and their ability to respond on their feet (Smith and Smith, 2008: 1).

Such workers are distinctive and have skills and qualities that set them apart. They have what Larry Parsons (2002) has described as a 'spark' that has been recognised and nurtured; they put others before themselves and have altruistic motivations. Many of these skills involved cannot be taught and are often overlooked as they are difficult to measure or define.

Throughout my journey I made many acquaintances, a few of whom I am honoured to call friends. Many of these people have contributed to the content of this chapter. There are others who offered me an insight into their personal struggle during my research. The majority of the people who contributed to this chapter promoted, and believed in, the importance of giving young people time and support to learn, grow and develop. Taking our own advice – allowing enough time to write and tweak assignments, managing our work life balance, enjoying the time we have, thinking, discussing and challenging our thoughts and actions, asking for help and support – would greatly assist us in our endeavours.

The nature of the struggle

While doing my research for this chapter it became apparent that individuals had difficulties articulating both how they felt, and the actual point with which they were struggling. This is a concept I understand! It is not surprising: after all, if we knew and understood what was happening then it would be easier to deal with – and less of a struggle!

The depth, breadth and nature of struggles are difficult to categories and articulate, but incorporate a range of emotive and practical aspects. These include:

- Balancing working life and home life.
- Engaging in study.
- Managing relationships – not only personal relationships, but also those with our agencies, work colleagues, families, study groups and young people.

As Heather Smith and Mark K. Smith (2008: 1) have commented:

> Workers have to balance considerable pressures arising from their work; their involvement in training and development; their personal life and relationships; and their involvement in communal affairs.

When workers spoke to me about struggle, they identified this as a 'problem' and indicated that if there was a problem in one area or aspect it is very likely to affect another. The 'struggle' is not isolated, nor is it surprising. We were involved in an approach to learning that is concerned with the whole person.

It affects all aspects of who we are. Such 'holistic learning' is both what we seek in our practice and what we experience in our training. It is an approach to learning that seeks to engage fully all aspects of the learner – mind, body and spirit. The underlying holistic principle is that a complex organism 'functions most effectively when all its component parts are themselves functioning and co-operating effectively' (Brainwaremap, 2009 after Heron, 1996).

When there is conflict within or between different aspects of our person, it can be a bitter pill to take. Knowing who you are at home (i.e. parent, spouse, carer) but not at work (colleague, manager, leader) or through study (student, practitioner, trainer) can cause feelings of unease and create uncertainty. Should there be a situation where you don't know who you are at any of these points there are increased pressures.

Attempting to get the correct or optimum 'fit', defining and knowing one's roles and responsibilities, in each variety of setting involves time and effort. This may involve sacrifice as well as adaptation. When we are at this point establishing, gaining and meeting expectations; managing change; and developing and moving on relationships – getting support that's right for us in the different roles can be difficult. But it can be done.

Many of the people to whom I spoke, noted the difficulty in discussing these pressures, and the public nature of struggle. Because something was difficult and different, it was given particular focus and they disliked this 'negative, under the microscope' attention. This initially made many of the workers reluctant to share. However, people often quickly realised that working in isolation is not productive. Social groupings provide an essential support network and can help us learn and grow.

By avoiding the exposure of our weaknesses, challenges and struggles, in fear of what people may think or say about us, we risk sacrificing the opportunity to gain – or learn – something. This feeling of fear and exposure is something that continues to challenge me in my working practice and aspects of my life. Although I believe that most decent people will acknowledge similar feelings or experiences and give credit – acknowledgement – praise for being human, admitting when there is a problem, and attempting to work through can be difficult. Often we may see someone who portrays a swan-like appearance (elegant on the surface, while underneath unknown to us they are frantically paddling/working to maintain this façade).

Throughout my research people made significant reference to 'who' they were with particular people. For example, when they were at home they were the parent, carer, provider; whichever role they played indicated who they would let 'in' regarding different aspects of themselves. They would not necessarily discuss personal problems with their young children, they would choose a particular friend or a partner. People would categorise themselves and discuss what they felt appropriate with those chosen people. This included a wide range of people including spouse/partner, children, priest/minister, parents, friends, colleagues.

There is an important point to be made here: if we don't engage in discussion to explore and break down the struggle, our chances of progress and success are minimal. More importantly the process of exploration and discussion are a release. They help us filter out concerns, gain perspective, prioritise, and give recognition to the intricacies of people's, feelings, learning and development. If we are looking to help and support others to grow and develop through informal and community education, then we must be able to put ourselves in those positions.

Growing as a practitioner and student

As youth workers we *offer* support for young people to explore and develop; as practitioners and students we *need* support to develop. Although it may be scary there are many people who can and will help us as we change. Choosing to ask for, and accepting, help is central to moving forward. We must put ourselves forward, and on the line, in order to seek this assistance. During my research people often talked about the difficulty of taking that first step. However, after taking the first step, things often become less scary or uncomfortable, and people feel less exposed and nervous.

Many who struggle can make significant links between youth work practice, knowing and understanding roles and responsibilities, and study. Wherever we begin our journeys – as volunteers, trainees, and part-time or full-time youth workers – we bring a certain level of ability. Our attendance and participation demonstrates to others that we care and make the effort. At varying stages in our journey as youth workers we have a particular level of ability – and it is essential that we know what that is – and where our limitations are.

Parker J. Palmer (1998: 10) has argued that educating others cannot be reduced to technique, but rather comes from the identity and integrity of the educator. It is, therefore, vital that we appreciate how we as people impact on others. However, there is something more: if we do not know who we are and what we think, then it is difficult to see how we can know others and the issues they face (Palmer 1998: 2; Smith and Smith, 2008: 20).

Using a tool such as Johari's window (developed by Joseph Luft and Harry Ingham) is a helpful way into examining our self awareness in these respects. Charles Handy (1999a: 63–71) has likened Johari's window to a house with four rooms. Room one is the part of ourselves that we see and others see. Room two is what others see but we are not aware of. Room three is the unconscious or subconscious bits of us seen neither by ourselves nor others. Last, room four is our private space. It is what we know but keep from others. How we view ourselves is an important part of our journey – we aspire to encourage young people to explore who they are and as their role model it would be fair to suggest that we have an understanding of ourselves.

We go through stages of self-discovery, which can be illustrated through the 'conscious competence ladder'. This theory suggests there are four states of consciousness and competence that people may pass through as they learn. Howell gives us an overview of these stages.

> *Unconscious incompetence* – this is the stage where you are not even aware that you do not have a particular competence. *Conscious incompetence* – this is when you know that you want to learn how to do something but you are incompetent at doing it. *Conscious competence* – this is when you can achieve this particular task but you are very conscious about everything you do. *Unconscious competence* – this is when you finally master it and you do not even think about what you have such as when you have learned to ride a bike very successfully (Howell, 1982: 29–33).

Knowing who we are, what we are capable of, and where we fit, is an important part of how we conduct ourselves. We are, after all, our own most important tool. When I began my journey I was happy that I was a trainee; I recognised that I had skills and that through the training they would grow. As a result, I tried to recognise and appreciate that others may be further on in their learning than I was in mine. Initially I would compare myself to others but, after a while I realised that should only compare myself to me. I am unique. I may have similarities, and traits that are the same as others, but I am me. For example, I thought I should respect other people's opinions, not wanting to offend or upset anyone. However, through a range of experiences, I came to realise that people were entitled to their opinions and that they should be respected as people, but that I don't have to respect their opinions – particularly if those opinions conflicted with my own or commonly held views.

Connecting theory and practice

Working and learning at the same time can be difficult, not only in terms of time management, but also with regard to fitting work around learning and learning around work. Are we focusing on connecting our practice to the theory or putting the theory into practice – which came first the chicken or the egg? Does it really matter? What does matter is that we are asking the questions, whether in our heads or out aloud, and trying to build our theory and practice.

Much of my struggle came from not verbalising the change in my role and responsibilities. I knew that I was having to make increasingly more complex decisions, but did not realise that my role was changing around me. As I became more capable, I would find myself in more difficult situations and, in order to produce the most effective solutions to problems, I began asking questions. Having additional information allowed me to form answers. Sometimes I made mistakes, but often the answer suited the situation.

Asking questions

A good friend of mine who was also on her own journey went to a conference. While in a discussion group she was faced with the situation of not knowing what it was the facilitator was talking about. She recalled thinking 'Should I ask her what she means and possibly look silly or should I let this go over my head?' On looking around her group the blank faces helped her choose her answer. Braving the fear she asked for clarification – beginning her sentence with 'This might sound like a stupid question but . . .' She was met with the response, 'Yes it does sound like a stupid question', and this prompted her to challenge the facilitator and again ask for clarification, stating how was she to participate if she did not understand what was being asked of her.' and not wanting to have her efforts to understand be in vain or for that matter be impeded by someone who would not help. The facilitator relented and broke down the terminology. After clarifying the matter my friend was proud of her tactful yet assertive approach to the situation. Since then she has maintained 'There are no such things as stupid questions – only stupid people: who don't ask enough questions'. Asking questions helps us work things through.

When attempting to gain information from colleagues and others they would often use jargon and complicated sounding words (often unknowingly

I think). Jargon and technical language can be a means of excluding people. Sometimes it is necessary but, if they or we can't break things down in order for others to engage in that situation, then there is a great danger of creating barriers. What is more, if we or others are not able to explain things clearly, do we or they really understand what is being talked about? Are we willing to ask 'What does it mean?' Or are we going to let others monopolise the situation.

Many people I spoke with when researching this Chapter commented on the pressures of appearing silly, foolish or stupid. There was also the fear of 'information overload', having so much information and far too many things to think about and put in to perspective. Their concern was that they would not see, or became/become unable to see, the wood for the trees. As a result it would be difficult to clarify points and make a decision, or come to an answer.

You only know what you know. In order to gain more information we need exposure: to people, situations to different subject areas. One of the key ways to gain new information is through conversation/dialogue/interaction. In engaging in this we get so much more than the information, we gain perspective, context, and empathy. This is an important point when working through our struggles: having the courage to say the words, to ask yourself and others questions, and to write down thoughts.

The overwhelming majority of those I spoke to had a range of people to talk with. The 'with' here is important. We are not talking *to* them we are talking *with* them: we have chosen these people as we feel we will gain something from them. Having a variety of people to discuss different aspects and elements with was an absolute essential. Indeed, the focus of this book is *Journeying Together* and this implies there are other travellers who are visiting and taking tours.

Our lives are full of incidental and purposeful meetings, the fact that we choose to share our journey creates friendships and associations offering not only a listening ear, but a response which can come from a caring heart, and knowledge and understanding of the environment in which the person operates. It may also be a response that helps us explore our values and beliefs. All this requires trust from ourselves to share with others what we think and feel, trusting someone to listen and respond – advising or commenting on deep and meaningful elements of our lives.

Exploring – and finding the right people

As part of my studies I was provided with a tutor, line manager and supervisor. Initially I did not know or understand what these people did and how they could help. I soon discovered that their role was to support me through supervision – although each role (tutor, supervisor, line manager) would offer help in a different fashion. Each would offer 'a central form of support where we can focus on our own difficulties as a worker' (Hawkins and Shohet, 2000: 23).

The tutor offered support via the role of *educator*, the external supervisor via the role of *provider of support*, and the line manager via the role of *managerial oversight* (*op. cit.*, 2000). I don't think I will ever be able to express how useful these roles were in helping me explore my working practice. Focusing on, and coming from, different aspects of my journey (work, practice and study) each of these roles provided a particular area of help for me. This is something to note, as we had different roles to play at different times. On study days, we played the role of student, during face-to-face sessions we are educators, while at home we may be partner or parent. We are one person playing a variety of roles. Managing these, and working out which role fits where, is an important part of our learning.

In addition to getting to know and understand our roles there can be additional pressures. While researching this chapter, workers also commented on the added struggle of working within the area where they live. While there can be very significant benefits in being local, it does create further pressures as workers grow, and change their attitude, behaviour and actions.

Many of those involved in the *Youth or Adult?* Initiative had either grown up in the areas where they were working or had lived there for some time. As a result, they had to both establish themselves in a new role as a full-time youth worker, and be accepted as they changed both within that role – and as people as they learn to appreciate and accept the values of the work they were doing. A number talked about the tensions involved in this – especially where the way they were now was in contrast to previous attitudes, behaviours and actions. This is given a further twist by the extent to which we, as local workers and educators, are dependent on being experienced as authentic and having integrity. For us to retain moral authority and to be experienced as 'real', we have to be consistent in who we are and how we act, wherever we are, at home or work (Jeffs and Smith, 2005: 94–109; Rogers, 1967).

Having support, time and space from those closest to us, as we continued on our journey, was described as a 'significant' part of the process. We have acknowledged the support from tutor, supervisor and line manager but others around us – work colleagues, family and friends – also play an important part. This they do by recognising and accepting who we are and what we are aspiring to achieve. Many practitioners reported that often family and friends knew or understood very little about what it is they are actually studying or facing within their work practice.

Local workers are not only on a journey; they are making significant choices, and dealing with emotional and complex developmental issues. This all takes its toll – and when this is combined with changes in our values and ways of thinking, together with the additional time spent studying – there can be significant extra strain on close relationships. Sometimes the strain is such that they break or become seriously weakened. We find ourselves drifting away from some old friends, or feeling that we don't have much to say to certain family members, or finding that we have to separate from partners. Each of us is on a journey and we turn to those around us and closest to us for help. They, hopefully, are able to give us their time, affection, space and help guide us along the way.

During my research, workers also talked about the significance of membership of formal and informal groups, and networks in terms of support (Zareena Abidi-Sheldon talks about this in Chapter 9). Some groups and networks are part of work and study situations, while others were more organic and 'natural'. Membership – and the relationships and conversations this entailed – often provided a significant drive to continue. Discovering who we can talk to, discussing a variety of situations with different people, can take time and be initially confusing.

Ultimately, there is the promise of clarity and understanding. Using supervision and those around us for support, can assist us to work through scenarios and problems in order to help us make sense of them. Nothing is ever simple – and finding the right person (or people) to discuss, explore and expose ourselves to takes time.

In conclusion

At one level we would not want the journey to be simple, because then it would not be as worthwhile. Everything that requires effort has an element of equity and satisfaction in reaping the rewards. People may think they want the simple life, but this is not possible if we are seeking to discover who we are.

Even now writing this chapter I have struggled – waiting till the last minute to ask for help and doing it at arms length via email, rather than picking up the phone or travelling to see the relevant person. After backing myself into a corner I was given a cheery and supportive response. I should have known this. Although this is a new aspect of my journey and I am like everyone else still discovering things, I hadn't fully learned from my experiences. This is why the journey never ends. It just makes different stops.

Much of the difficulty with personal struggle was, and is, a reluctance to speak to someone – to admit that you're not where you want to be, that you need help! This is one of the most important things that I learned as part of my journey. By broaching the subject or raising concerns, people are nearly always supportive (once you find the right people for you then this becomes even easier). My supervisors and tutors were exceptionally skilled in helping me to help myself and to learn through the process of conversation and exploration of practice.

Throughout my struggles I knew I had someone to talk with and be honest about what I was thinking and feeling. They did not tell me the answers; they assisted me in clarifying and searching out further information. I often disliked it when they (tutor/supervisor) would not tell me the answer. However, when I reached the next point in my journey, I was able to draw on points of view and questions they had posed. This helped me realise that finding 'the answer' is not all its cracked up to be, that it was how I approach situations and my responses to the things that are thrown at me that are more important. And 'solutions' take shape from engaging with that process.

My struggle was a process of discovery and progression, which better equipped me for the next challenge. It gave me a sense of achievement. It reminds me that growing as a person, and increasing my confidence and abilities as an informal and community educator was, and remains, well worth working for.

Questions for reflection

- We often sacrifice gaining something through not exposing our weaknesses and challenges and struggles in fear of what people may think or say about us. Has this been the case for you with regard to exploring the way you work? How have you overcome this fear, what more could you be doing?

- So much of what we do as youth workers and informal educators is wrapped up with the people we are. This makes development a struggle. What things are you having to face at the moment? How are you going about dealing with them?

- Think about your experiences of finding support to explore questions arising out of your practice, and around you as a worker. Do you have the right people around you now? Are there others that you can identify who might be able to offer support?

CHAPTER 7

Implications for, and impacts on, the organisation

Kai Wooder

This chapter explores the impact that different forms of funding can have on an agency. I look at the experience of working with a funder that sees what they are doing as an investment – and what that has meant for those involved.

Money, money, money

Accessing funding is pretty much at the top of the list of priorities for voluntary and charitable organisations. We need money to invest in our beliefs, values, programmes and projects. We need money to pay staff, to pay the rent and to pay the bills. We need money. Money is not the root of all evil, money rocks. We need money. Without money there are no projects, no planned social interventions, no working towards justice for all, no challenging negative societal beliefs and no staff to pay. We need money.

When we receive information telling us that funding is available for some piece of work, we often decide without too much thought, that the opportunity cannot go a-begging. This work then becomes a new focus and priority for the organisation.

The mistake that we are often at risk of making is in not considering the impact funding can have on the organisation. Does it support the organisation's values? Does it support the organisation's plans? It's a difficult dilemma for voluntary organisations and sometimes it feels like it would be better not to ask the questions at all. If we don't ask then we don't have to deal with the fact that we might be sourcing money that goes against what we believe and what we really want to do. No. It seems the only option is to apply for the money and then make it work for us. After all, it is better that we have the money than not have it. We need money.

Looking to outcomes

The situation is common and frustrating. Funders usually want to give money in return for outcomes. For the most part these are set by the funder – not by the organisation or local people – and they usually relate to a specific agenda.

When the funding comes via a government source, you can bet your bottom dollar it will relate to getting young people off the streets; getting young people into jobs; getting young people to be quiet after 8 p.m.; getting young people not to drink; getting young people not to take drugs; or getting young people not to have sex. These are real outcomes; they are tangible, recordable and visible. If the world were a circus, these outcomes would be the strong men of all performers, real crowd pleasers, with a full house of paying customers every day of the week. If you have set your organisation up to uphold and support these outcomes then all is good, you probably have a long and prosperous future ahead. If, however, your organisation exists to encourage young people to explore their values, to support personal development, to raise aspirations and promote informed yet autonomous decision-making . . . you might be feeling some tension.

It's a difficult situation. We can see that some of the outcomes that the potential funder wants may, in fact, be supportive of young people and communities. This is particularly evident within my own field of sexual health. Most current government outcomes relate to a reduction in sexually transmitted infections amongst young people, as well as decreasing the rate of unplanned pregnancies. As an overall strategy the outcomes are desirable and would serve to improve young people's health and well-being. The conflict lies in the ethos and belief of autonomy. We may well work to encourage more informed decision-making, more access to sexual health information and services, but we also know that we cannot guarantee the actions of others and that freedom of thought and of choice may well lead to different outcomes. In reality, some of the outcomes are not ours to promise, we can certainly work to encourage them but we cannot assure them. You could:

(a) Take the money and hope that the outcomes match.
(b) Take the money and use your creative integrity.
(c) Take the money and make sure that the outcomes match.
(d) Not take the money and risk the future of the organisation.

The choice is yours. What is clear is that when we guarantee outcomes we take something very special away from the ethos of informal education, voluntary association and the right to choose.

Tony Jeffs and Mark K Smith (2008: 280) explore this issue in their paper, *Valuing Youth Work*:

> While there is talk of local services setting their own curriculum and developing their own plans, one of the inescapable features of new frameworks is that agencies have to address centrally-defined targets and indicators. The rise of commissioning has strengthened this.

They go on to address the impact of outcome-related funding by saying, 'The result has been the significant fall in the degree of freedom that state-employed and state-funded workers have to respond to the needs and wishes of the young people they encounter, or the wider communities in which they are located' (op. cit.).

Ideally, we would be funded to work with young people in a way that underpins choice, relationships and freedom. If the voluntary sector were in the circus then youth workers would be funded to spin plates – lots and lots of plates! We would be top of the bill, cheered and applauded for dropping a few, keeping others going, not giving up, passing some of the plates to other people and growing more arms when the situation required it.

As we work in a culture of outcomes, vulnerability and uncertainty, the challenge is to think through the implications and impact that any amount of funding could have on your organisation. It is then to decide if you can handle it, if you can manage it and if, in doing so, you can stay true to your values.

In our agency we have found it useful to determine our own outcomes prior to meeting with funders by making an assessment of how our work is likely to contribute towards the achievement of government targets, rather than adopting them as our own. We can then describe how our work *could* impact on a national target – for example, increasing the testing and treatment rates for Chlamydia – rather than guarantee the success, in terms of specific numbers and statistics. This approach has enabled us to focus on particular areas of defined government targets that we honestly believe our work supports, thus giving us the best chance of staying true to our work. It also shows funders that we are committed to the bigger picture, whilst maintaining the reality of our role within it. This is not easy, but we know that it is also possible to be funded and still keep the heart of the organisation.

One thing is for certain though. *Don't take the money if you're not prepared to change.* Money changes things, sometimes for the better and sometimes for the worse. Done right, money enables organisations to grow and, thus, enables youth work to grow.

Funding as an investment in people, places and communities

Some funders, thankfully, take another path. They look for organisations that are in touch with local realities and that they can trust to develop work that meets the needs they have identified. Crucially, they also invest in training – looking not only to develop the work, but also the worker – and involve workers, managers and young people in a wider network.

In the current climate funders, like the Rank Foundation, who work in this way, are viewed as pioneering, fantastic and remarkable. But if we unhook ourselves from what Seddon (2008) has shown to be an irrational belief in targets, and 'deliverology', an approach to funding that listens to what local people and organisations are saying – and then invests in them – makes sense.

When money is provided as an investment to grow local youth work in local communities, rather than a cheque handed over in return for outcomes achieved, it makes for flexibility in approach and innovation. In our experience, it raises morale – especially as it makes it more possible to respond to the real and current needs of young people. Unfortunately, this approach is in contrast to most other funders – and it throws their approaches into sharp relief. If, for example, we were in a sweet shop, such funders would say 'I will give you £500 and in return I would like 1000 limited edition chocolate bars, individually counted and delivered gift wrapped . . . and I'd like them by Monday. Oh, and don't forget the paperwork'. An investor would say 'I will give you £500 and in return I would like to see your shop continue to thrive and for your customers to be happy'. The money is the same yet the approach and the ethos is very different. The focus of the funding is on the process of working with young people and communities, and in return it will produce outcomes. These outcomes should be useful, affirming and positive for young people and for communities, the only difference being that we can grow with them and in turn, ensure their relevance.

This is not to say there won't be problems along the way, there will, but it's important that we face them as equal partners and with a genuine desire for a solution. Mistakes will be made, the direction of work will change. However, in an approach that looks to investment, there is something much closer to partnership. Where the concern is to commission and contract services, the relationship between funder and local agency is far more unequal.

Where investment lies at the core, funders and agencies take a shared responsibility for the work and for its development. We don't walk away when the going gets tough and we also stay true to the process and the learning. When funders don't view organisations as equal partners and *vice versa*, there is a potential to overlook the process and, in turn, reduce its potential to make a real difference to young people's lives and local communities.

The National Council for Voluntary Organisations (NCVO) has provided some insight into current relationship between funders and organisations. The situation has not changed in any significant way since they carried out their consultation around developing a strategy for performance improvement in 2004. Then they found that short-term funding settlements and resistance to full cost recovery made it hard for voluntary and community organisations to implement sustainable performance improvement.

> . . . funders often require organisations to have particular quality standards in place before accessing funding. These are often imposed and are rarely negotiated. Funders can have unrealistic expectations about what quality standards could achieve and how quickly they bring about service improvements.

They continue:

> The funding environment should enable voluntary and community or-ganisations to succeed, not hinder them. This means a more mature relationship between funded and funder, with funders respecting the independence of those they fund, and with funded organisations better understanding the context of those who fund them.

The experience of investment – a case study

Working for an organisation that has achieved long term funding (five years) from a funder who wants to invest in youth work by means of choice and positive association rather than concrete outcomes, has provided us with a platform for growth. The impact has been massive and our learning thus far has been huge.

One of the trickiest situations we have faced is that one worker is funded via the 'investors' money and the remaining four via the 'commissioners' money. All five staff work for the same organisation; all five staff share the agency's values in relation to young people, confidentiality and sexual health;

all five staff work within the same context and with the same aims; all five staff work the same hours and are managed by the same person. Why then, does it feel so different?

Contrasting experiences

Gaining the investment brought us joy, joy, joy. It enabled us to employ a local worker for five years. Not only that, she would have the opportunity to study via a distance learning route leading to a BA Honours Degree in Informal and Community Education. We were all so pleased.

The worker we employed was a young woman who had previously worked part-time on our reception desk and as an advisor to young people who came in to talk about their sexual health. She had shown amazing promise and potential, a complete understanding and support for the values of the agency and of youth work. She had a desire to join the education team and to really improve the quality of services offered to young people around sexual health, relationships and sexuality.

There was not an issue with her standard of work or commitment to Brook. The issue arose when she began taking one day per week as study time – which was part of the investment that the funder had made. Other staff noticed this and instead of viewing it as a working day for the new worker, appeared to see it as a day off. To be honest, initially, the worker also viewed it as a day off which probably didn't help the situation. Next came the brand new lap-top, then the books to help with the college course, then the trips away to conferences in lovely hotels. Next came the meetings in London, then there were two college residential courses to prepare for, then a glossy annual report to produce, then the free leadership course in the Lake District as well as the possibility of a full time funded volunteer, bursaries aplenty for further development opportunities and the fact that she was part of a national network of youth workers. All part of the investment – phew!

It is difficult not to be jealous of that level of support, investment and opportunity. I'm even envious of it. Natural reactions dictated a feeling of envy. This included judgements about whether or not the worker was worthy of the opportunity (maybe she's too young?) about her integrity towards study (was she using those days to study or to sleep?) and about her role within the team (was she part of the team or on the edge of it?). This was all completely unfair on the worker. All she was guilty of was applying for a job, getting it and accepting it. At the same time the situation felt very unfair on the other workers; why couldn't they study for one day a week, have proper resources, attend meetings, go to conferences, have new experiences? The reason of course is money.

Initially I would defend the worker and her situation, 'Look, she is funded differently, we have to accept that her situation is unique' I would say. It wasn't until speaking to other managers within the network that I realised that by accepting her situation as different and by assuming that the rest of the team should be tolerant of that situation was a poor judgement on my behalf. Not just poor, but apathy inducing.

The challenge – keeping the team together

The challenge to all organisations is to view the offer made by a long-term investment, in our case from the Rank Foundation, as an aspiration for all, rather than a unique situation. Increasing the opportunity for training, for resources, for networking, for reading and for learning across the whole organisation should become the next challenge. We need to source opportunities for other staff within the team; we need to show that we are as committed to their development as we are to the funded worker.

In reality it is very hard, maybe even unlikely, that we can ever match the investment by the funder and extend it to other members of the team, but we will aspire to do just that. We have started to work towards this aim and along the way have discovered ways to use funding to support this. For example; we have encouraged staff to study funding the fees and staff using their own time for study. Because of the funding we already have a library of books that the worker used the previous year and which now becomes a training resource for other members of staff. When bursaries arise, particularly for leadership courses, we ask for two places and while it's not always possible to have them, sometimes we can and then a further member of staff can also attend some funded training along with the funded worker. This has been so useful, especially in bringing the ethos and values of investing in youth work into the wider team and for us all to view the investment in the worker as an investment in the agency, and therefore in us all.

Managing the relationships

In order to survive a five-year relationship, particularly when that relationship is open and involves multiple and sometimes strange partners, a water-tight strategy is required. Very early on we realised that, as in life, it is near impossible to keep a number of partners happy at the same time. It's exhausting. One thing we could do though was remain open to learning and stay committed to dialogue as a way of moving forward. Dialogue can be an interesting concept and when you have many partners including a long term investor, a college, a manager, a supervisor, a tutor and a UK wide network, the potential for misunderstanding is high.

Dialogue is, of course, a conversation – although, at times people confuse conversations with monologues. This is easy to do, especially when you have a great story to share, but it can also be unproductive and, let's face it, a bit boring for the listener. With so many partners in our lives the key to remaining interested and productive was for us to work out how the lines of communication worked between so many people. This is what we learnt:

- *The funder talks to the agency, the agency talks to the funder.* This relationship has been consistent and positive. The funder include 'managers' in every aspect of their communication with new workers including conferences, handbooks, network meetings, opportunities.
- *The worker talks to the funder and agency (and vice versa) all of the time.* Some organisations struggle with the idea of the worker speaking directly to the funder but it is all part of the process of investment in youth work. It supports transparency and ensures that relationships are more equal.
- *The funder talks to the college, the college talks to the funder.* The funder and the college have a long and positive relationship. The college are also invited to attend events, conferences and meetings.
- *The agency can talk to college, the college can talk to agency – but it doesn't happen often.* In this approach – that is based in relationships of trust – there are very few reasons why an agency would need to talk to the college. This doesn't mean that there is no communication. For example, the college provides agencies with information and support on the worker/ student's course work and assessments.
- *The worker (student) talks to college, the college talks to worker (student).* It is sometimes easy to forget that the worker is also a student. The worker/students relationship with the college is important, especially when the course is via a distance learning route.

It took some time, but we realised that within open and multiple relationships, some people have more dialogue than others and some partners hardly speak to each other at all. It works because we know that our professional values are similar and our desire to journey together through the whole process is the same. It also helps when dialogue is effective.

Making dialogue effective

Dialogue (or conversation) as Gadamer has argued, is a process of two people understanding each other. As such it is inherently risky and involves questioning our beliefs and assumptions.

> Thus it is a characteristic of every true conversation that each opens himself to the other person, truly accepts his point of view as worthy of consideration and gets inside the other to such an extent that he understands not a particular individual, but what he says. The thing that has to be grasped is the objective rightness or otherwise of his opinion, so that they can agree with each other on a subject (Gadamer, 1979: 347).

The concern is not to 'win the argument', but to advance understanding and human well-being. Agreement cannot be imposed, but rests on common conviction (Habermas, 1984: 285–7). As a social relationship it entails certain virtues and emotions.

The views of Gadamer and Habermas also relate to the education thinker Paulo Freire's (1972) beliefs that learning is a social activity. He believed that you can't do someone's learning for them but equally you can't learn without them. Learning is social, it occurs through conversation and in groups. This is true of our learning so far. We have had to make time for dialogue, time for thinking things through, time to 'sleep on things' and time to come to one conclusion only to disregard it and start again. 'Investment funding' and having a worker who is also a student has brought this new learning to us. It has made us value this time as valuable time and to see it as a learning process.

Relationships

New relationships also tend to raise some questions, thoughts and concerns. Is this the right relationship for me? Am I happy? Am I ready? What do they want me to sign? Organisational readiness will certainly be tested here and this does have an impact. Writing a funding proposal can encourage us to promise all kinds of things but the prospect of seeing them all through can be daunting. Being ready in this situation is more of a mind-set than a checklist of competencies.

In our relationship with the worker, the agency and the college, being ready meant being open to new experiences, being willing to meet new people and share knowledge, supporting a new worker who was about to embark on a massive journey and most astonishingly, be ready to work with a funder who will view you as an equal partner and be flexible to your needs. This did take some getting used to. It's funny now but initially I think we were a little bit suspicious of funder and their apparently 'peculiar' ways. We tried to work out what their motives could be and held a slightly defensive posture for a while.

In truth, the funder did want something from us in return for their investment. This included an honest relationship with us, and participation in conversations, events and the wider network of projects (*yarn*, described further in Chapters 8–10). They also wanted us to recognise young leaders in our communities and for us to support their growth and development. They want our organisation to thrive and for the young people involved to be happy. They wanted us to do things at our own pace and they wanted to get to know you, your organisation and your work. What we found was that this funder was not strange, but different. Their belief in youth work and in young people challenged us to reassess our values and standards. All this has encouraged us to open our minds to the notion of 'team' as being more than the people we see, meet and talk with.

The writer and strategist Peter Senge has developed our thinking about 'learning organisations' through his vision that learning involves a group of people who are constantly developing their own capabilities in order to create new possibilities. Senge highlights the notion of 'team' as being central to this;

> When you ask people about what it is like being part of a great team, what is most striking is the meaningfulness of the experience. People talk about being part of something larger than themselves, of being connec-ted, of being generative. It become quite clear that, for many, their experiences as part of truly great teams stand out as singular periods of life lived to the fullest. Some spend the rest of their lives looking for ways to recapture that spirit (Senge, 1990: 13).

In our case, when you meet a worker/agency and they tell you that they have or are funded by The Rank Foundation, you feel able to converse with the confidence that some of your experiences will be shared. Similarly, when you meet a worker and they tell you that they have studied or are studying with the YMCA George Williams College, you feel able to ask them about people, places and concepts. In short, you feel part of a wider and bigger team. You feel able to talk to strangers on a deeper level because your learning is shaped by each others, you have an instant history. This is priceless.

To be or not to be . . .

Within all relationships personality has a key role to play. Often in work situations we adopt the 'personality' of the organisation, especially when attending meetings, speaking at events, meeting new people etc. We adopt the language, ethos and reputation of the organisation and become its voice.

The word 'personality' originates from the Latin *persona*, which means mask, not a mask in the sense of 'covering up or hiding' a set of individual characteristics but a mask to represent and embody a character. The challenge, within a long-term and sometimes social relationship, is to try and be true to both personalities; that of yours and of the organisation. It can feel like you're walking a fine line at times, but I believe that the relationship between the agency, the worker, the manager, the funder and the college is a lot deeper than many other external associations. Although the personality of the organisation is important, the personalities of the worker and manager are equally so. You are encouraged to have opinions, differences, ideas and dilemmas – in fact, I would say you are *expected* to have them and to communicate and engage in discourse with others. Relationships work best when the mask isn't hiding a person but *representing* them.

The impact and implications of long term 'investment funding', in our experience, are plentiful and also ongoing. The one most consistent impact is that of change. Change is inevitable and funding changes things. The organisation will change and adapt to meet this new challenge, the worker/ student will certainly change and grow and learn, the manager will need to change and adapt to the new learning that is going on around them. The challenge is to face that change with integrity and personality and as an equal partner in the process.

Marcel Proust said that 'one of the great and wonderful characteristics about good books' is the way 'our own wisdom begins where that of the author leaves off' (see de Botton, 1998). Good books encourage us to start our own thinking but should not encourage us to see our learning as complete. I hope your journey is challenging and also surprising.

Acknowledgement

This chapter is a glimpse into our experiences in one agency, but has also been developed from the knowledge and conversations with other agencies, workers, students and managers from across the Rank network. Special thanks to all workers from across The Rank Foundation network (*yarn*), especially those who gave particular insight for this chapter; Mike Burns from CAIR Scotland, Jeane Lowe from Centre 63 and Harriet, Viccie and the team at Wirral Brook.

Questions for reflection

- Reflect on the experience you have had of an agency applying for funding that alters the focus of the work. What changes were involved and how did the character of the work change?
- Dealing with contrasting requirements and expectations from different funders is now a significant area of work for many of us. What issues have arisen for you, and what lessons can be learnt for the future development of the agency.
- Having funding that is seen as an investment has both benefits and costs. It demands a different way of working. Reflect on what might be involved and how it might impact on some of the work you are currently involved in.

CHAPTER 8

Creating and sustaining a philosophy for development

Simon Hill

The ethical principles of work with young people are based on respect. I argue that for youth work to flourish and develop that sense of respect needs to exist throughout the people and organisations supporting the front line work.

Consistency of values creates and sustains work that develops young people, workers and agencies. The 'journeying together' approach is an attempt to create that consistency. In this chapter I give a worker/student's perspective on that approach and the relationships involved.

Quotations in this chapter are taken from conversations with youth workers.

Youth work principles

Intrinsic to the nature of youth work is a belief in young people and an understanding that they are more likely to flourish, where they are treated with respect and trust is placed in them. The National Youth Agency recognises this in their ethical principles statement, which commits youth workers to:

1. Treat young people with respect, valuing each individual and avoiding negative discrimination.
2. Respect and promote young people's rights to make their own decisions and choices, unless the welfare or legitimate interests of themselves or others are seriously threatened.

3. Promote and ensure the welfare and safety of young people, while permitting them to learn through undertaking challenging educational activities.
4. Contribute towards the promotion of social justice for young people and in society generally, through encouraging respect for difference and diversity and challenging discrimination (NYA, 2004).

These goals and principles underpin youth work and help to define its purpose. Work based on these values is demanding. The nature of the work brings with it another inevitable question and challenge: 'what setting is required, in order to grow and develop work that meets those ethical requirements?'

The *Youth or Adult?* experience is built on the premise that work will flourish where the relationships supporting the face-to-face work are built on those same values. The respect and trust must flow across management, organisation and, ideally, through to the funding body. Indeed, the funding body has a fundamental influence in setting that climate.

Pebbles in the pond

The Rank Foundation is based on the values of J. Arthur Rank. 'Pebble in the pond' is the strap-line of the organisation and this reflects the ethos of the initiative, which stems from the attitude of J. Arthur and his belief in young people. His focus was on recognising leadership and realising potential (Cowen, 2003).

The pebble is the initial investment in the individual, who is then nurtured and encouraged on their journey. The ripples from this 'pebble in the pond' are the effects of this investment, which have significant consequences for the life of the individual worker, the community in which they are based and the young people with whom they work. As one worker realises:

> *I am the pebble in the pond. Rank invested in me, it was a great privilege to be given that opportunity. That was the start of my personal development, building the connections in the community, building those relationships: an investment in the individual, not the organisation. The ripple effect involved me in putting something back through training. People were doing the youth work but needed training.*

Another worker puts it like this:

For me the pebble in the pond is letting individuals or organisations fulfil something of their potential. Instead of seeing young people as targets or outcomes, workers ask them to look at who they are and what they want to achieve. These workers come with such passion, they look to potential.

This approach demonstrates a genuine faith in people. The funders put their trust in the workers and release them to do the work – work that focuses on processes and relationships, rather than 'targets and outcomes'. It's a bold and perhaps scary process for all involved – to put all of that belief into one person. But the art of investment is in recognising individuals in organisations who have the potential to succeed.

The rest of this chapter analyses this approach to investment, with a view to understanding the key elements that make it effective in creating and sustaining a developmental approach to work with young people that fulfils the principles of good practice. There are three key elements:

- Sufficient *time* is given for the process to have an impact; this will be considered here as **'The journey'**.
- The *supportive framework* for the worker – **'Together – the relationship'**.
- The *relationship* with the worker helps to evaluate progression and creates new opportunities for the future – **'Journeying together'**.

This analysis, based on the experience of the *Youth or Adult?* programme, provides valuable lessons for the wider field.

The journey

A journey is often a vehicle by which people discover themselves. When young people go on a journey to discover themselves, we could be of help to them if we could accompany them, sometimes physically, sometimes in spirit (Green and Christian, 1998: 13).

The *Youth or Adult?* journey is a significant one, taking place across five years and involving many changes in the lives of the workers.

When I first started on this journey, I'd just moved to a new town and started a new job. Over time my job changed as the project became more established, and my role moved from worker to manager. However, there were lots of personal changes too. At the end of my qualification, I was engaged to be married, something I could not have envisaged at the start!

All of my fellow students experienced similarly dramatic changes – marriages, divorces, births of children, moving home – life-changing events which had an impact on our lives, both personally and professionally.

As a student there is a lot of pressure, expectations from the college, the employer. There is also a lot break-up in relationships, you can lose friends and have problems in your family.

Just as I might look back on my time at school or University as a significant time in my life, so my involvement with Rank frames a substantial period of growth and development. The relationship with others in the Rank network has been for me, and I know for others, a great source of support during these times.

For one worker, this journey is defined by one word:

The word 'growth' – of the worker, the individual. It is also because of the five years. It is five years work with young people. There is a lot of growth involved. People kept asking me 'what do you think?' – now I ask other people that all the time!

Five years

Youth work is concerned with relationships; relationships take time to establish and bear fruit. Five years allows that time, and the Rank Charities use the time to nurture those relationships with workers. The workers are then liberated to establish effective relationships with young people, demonstrating commitment over a key transitional phase in their lives.

When I first started working in Bournemouth, I met a group of young people during a detached work session on a local council estate. As I introduced myself as a new youth worker, one of the first things they asked me was: 'how long are you here for?' Behind this question lay a scepticism rooted in their experience of youth workers thus far. So many times, they had been introduced to workers who made all sorts of promises, only to then be let down as these workers moved on to other projects. I was able to say, 'I'm here for five years,' which drew a rather astonished reaction. It was extremely important for me, establishing good working relationships in that community, that they knew I had the time to invest in them and through that time, the relationship, based on trust, was built.

The five years enables more than a 'quick fix' solution, but rather sees significant changes in communities lived out through a shared journey.

Faith and risk

The organisation I work for was struggling – living hand to mouth – it has been a lifeline. The knock on effect of investing in the person has allowed us to get further funding and to become better at what we do.

So often youth projects struggle for funding – always applying for the next grant or contract and trying to fit the aims of their work into the increasingly targeted focus of the funder's particular area of interest. An investment of five years comes as an enormous relief – and becomes a great opportunity. A five-year investment creates the potential to look further ahead, to develop initiatives that meet the needs identified within communities, rather than those defined externally.

The appeal of a journey is often in the freedom it represents – the chance to discover, grow and learn. Workers appreciate this opportunity:

It's a journey of personal development and of work. You change and they support it and allow for it.

A lot of people I talk to think Rank are mad. No one else funds like this. Why do they do it? It's a wise investment because you grow and the work deepens. The investment brings a return.

The risk of this approach is that workers may not last the five years – that some of the funding will be wasted. It's a risk many organisations are not prepared to make. Yet to have faith in people always involves risk. The belief shown in them makes workers feel valued and it encourages a commitment, which in time yields a return. Managers also recognise the value of this investment approach, which helps them to begin to think further ahead:

From a management point of view it stops a short-termist approach, it makes you think about a long-term strategy and not to get over-involved in fire-fighting. We have planning days now thinking: where are we going to go over the next five years? You have to think about what you are actually going to do in this community.

Another important aspect about this five-year commitment is that it allows for people to make mistakes. Again the element of risk is clear, but this commitment encourages the workers to take leaps of faith in their own projects and – importantly – to learn from them. When workers were asked to identify the changes on their journey with Rank, one worker recognised the . . .

> . . . *increased ability to learn from mistakes. Projects are encouraged to take risks and to allow mistakes – and to look at the learning from that.*

So often mistakes are viewed as failure and that leads to no further investment. The Rank strategy allows workers to admit their mistakes and identify what they have learned through that experience.

> *In Rank it is about the process, and learning from the process.*

Through an integral training process and through the support network built up through that, as well as within individuals' own organisations, mistakes can be talked through and viewed as part of the natural progression on this journey.

Together – the relationship

The *Youth or Adult?* scheme involves a four-way relationship between funder, youth worker, local agency and trainer. Rank approves the funding of the youth worker, who is then placed at the centre of this relationship. The workers in training form the key link between the Foundation's representatives, the wider network and the local community. The scheme also introduces the worker to the training body; staff from the YMCA George Williams College form a crucial part of the whole support network.

The interaction between the four partners forms a unique relationship, where all meet regularly and can have an open dialogue.

> *The way they form their relationships earns people's respect. People involved constantly talk about Rank, because they do not dictate to you and tell you what to do. They trust you and you go that extra mile. They believe in me more than I believe in myself. They keep on believing in me which is really making me believe in myself. It is a very special relationship.*

A unique relationship

When a worker joins the *Youth or Adult?* programme they enter into a relationship with the Rank Foundation in the broadest sense, able to tap into all of the resources that the charity offers.

Aside from the unique access to all levels of the Foundation, the relationship is sustained through the training offered by the YMCA George Williams College. The training takes the student on a journey. The ethos of the College and the funder match, through their understanding of informal education; workers have identified this and often refer to Rank or the College interchangeably:

> *It has reinforced the values of informal education. There is also an external accountability and a discipline via the framework that the student is learning through at the College.*
>
> *It is good the way the Foundation and the College work together. You have a key contact in Rank and the College is small enough to value you as an individual. The partners are quite honest, have regular reviews, and change things.*

The College ethos and practice also places the worker at the centre of their learning, so this relationship becomes very empowering. There could be a sense of Rank checking up on student's progress, through their relationship with YMCA personnel. However, this has never been my experience, as the relationship maintains professional boundaries, which enable the worker to draw on different people for different needs.

> *The partnership is fairly distinctive – each party is valued and has its own independence. External supervision is important.*

An equal partnership

There is also no real sense of hierarchy between the partners. On the face of it, the funder could be viewed as an external body, in their relationship to the worker and their agency. They hold the purse strings and could exercise power and authority through this – holding something over workers and projects, which forces them to achieve. In practice, however, workers feel they are on a level playing field, being treated as equals. The trust placed in workers, and freedom given to them develops a reciprocal level of commitment:

> *You don't want to let them down, the trust and respect has made me what I am. I got me, the organisation got a fantastic project.*

Workers feel valued for who they are. There is recognition that each project employs different workers with unique skills and ideas:

> *I really think that Rank treat people as individuals. They know what is going on for people. It is not just a treadmill. It's the core of youth work. Chris and Charlie [Rank Directors] are good at making you feel valued, that you have a role to play.*

This sense of value in individuals filters through to the workers face to face work with young people:

Where does it feed through into practice? I will never play the numbers game; nor do fall into the trap of 'mission drift'. The funding sees young people as people, not as 'units of consumption', 'output' or 'customers'.

A family

A sense of equality between Rank, workers and their agencies strengthens this unique relationship, building commitment and trust, so that the feeling is closer to being part of a family than an organisation.

A real level of trust – even the way you get the money upfront – and it is five years commitment. I can't remember anyone – other than my parents – who have had that belief in me!

Through this relationship there is an understanding that the worker invests more than just their professional life into the partnership, but instead the whole person becomes involved. Where Rank brings their funding and experience to the worker, the worker also invests their self into the process.

This holistic approach fosters a sense of collaboration rather than competition between different agencies associated with Rank:

A holistic way of thinking seeks to encompass and integrate multiple layers of meaning and experience rather than defining human possibilities narrowly (Miller, 2000).

The collaborative way of working encourages a breadth of experience throughout the network, which is shared between partners and helps individual workers feel part of something bigger.

Through being part of a network, workers gain a broader understanding of the youth work profession and new opportunities arise through the relationships that are created. There are many examples of workers sharing their learning, and helping each other – a process which has recently been identified and encouraged through the formation of *yarn* (Rank's informal network of funded workers and agencies) and its website (www.rankyouthwork.org) which promotes dialogue throughout the year, rather than just at Rank network events.

The holistic approach also recognises that youth work is more than a profession; it is a vocation – a calling that involves the whole person. Larry

Parsons recognised this and called for something of the volunteer in all youth workers.

> While professionalism has come to stay, if not salted with the devotion and selflessness of the volunteer, bureaucracy can become a dead hand which stifles initiative and kills the personal touch (Parsons, 2002: 17).

This view of youth work, as something bigger than a 'job', demands more than job descriptions can encompass. From the very top of the organisation; the Rank executive team give far more than could be expected. This volunteering mentality gives the Foundation the family feel that so many workers recognise. It is a refreshing alternative to a target-driven and tick-box approach, so evident elsewhere.

Journeying together

At the heart of the investment philosophy is the need to allow workers the chance to grow on their journey and to create the right environment for that to happen, through relationships. Beyond this lies a particular approach to evaluation, which measures the success of the scheme and the effectiveness of the workers. The approach relies on the personal and professional relationships between all of those involved on 'the journey'.

Evaluation through relationship

Often, youth work is measured in hard outcomes – boxes need to be ticked, and young people are passed on to other agencies:

> *Work is often defined by the form and the paperwork in the statutory sector. That needs turning around.*

There is a sense of frustration that youth work is not always valued as a profession in its own right – there's always a need to justify it. In Joanne Rowland's study, she identifies an alternative approach to evaluation, based on dialogue and enquiry rather than harder methods such as reports and presentations. In this approach:

> Evaluation is viewed as an integral part of the development or change process and involves 'reflection-action'. Subjectivity is recognised and appreciated (Rowlands cit. in Smith, 2001).

The YMCA George Williams College course promotes reflective practice, which encourages individuals constantly to evaluate their own work, as well as to understand themselves and how personality affects work. This reflection leads to change:

> . . . *the College puts a lot of theory in. If I wasn't reflective I would became stagnant and it has a knock-on effect on the communities we serve.*

This approach empowers the worker to recognise that they are involved in the process – they can talk to the funder about what they want to achieve:

> The evaluator takes on the role of facilitator, rather than being an objective and neutral outsider. Such evaluation may well be undertaken by 'insiders' – people directly involved in the project or programme (Rowlands cit. in Smith, 2001).

> *We tell Rank what we think should happen and Rank allows and supports it. Too often funders are all about targets and numbers. We are there for the long-term and we believe.*

There is an acceptance that Rank understands youth work. There are opportunities to meet and talk to the Rank directors. They visit projects and encourage workers to connect with others who work in similar communities.

At annual conferences, workers and managers from different projects mix with each other in small group discussions to reflect on their work and offer support and advice to each other. Each year, projects submit a report, but these are flexible documents that allow workers to communicate the work of their project in their own way.

Internal versus External

The educational reformist and philosopher John Dewey identified a difference between the physiological and the sociological in young people. He recognised that there is something natural in each person – a life-force or a spark. He calls on educators to sense what the individual has to offer and use their life experiences and talents as a guide to their education.

Too often, a set curriculum denies the differences in individuals. Dewey argues for a philosophical shift to recognise the individual and tailor education to suit their needs.

If we eliminate the social factor from the child we are left only with an abstraction; if we eliminate the individual factor from society, we are left only with an inert and lifeless mass (Dewey, 1897: 361–2).

At the same time, Dewey called for a renewed sense of community, where educational institutions create a sense of togetherness and create a greater lever of understanding of how we should live and learn together. There can be a tension between these two dynamics – nurturing the internal personality and ambition of the person versus shaping the external social environment that frames their living and learning. How can education be tailored to the individual and yet enhance a community experience?

The long-term investment approach to funding youth work manages this balance well, and enables both things to happen. It means that it is possible to nurture the spark of the individual, through support and encouragement. Workers have the freedom to develop projects that reflect the needs of their local communities.

At the same time, a supportive network ensures that training is in place. Workers develop their reflective practice and understanding of values within a wider community of practitioners. Returning to Dewey's theory, individual talent is coupled with the provision of a supportive community.

Workers appreciate this way of working and develop the same skills in their own projects – the ability to assist young people to develop their own individuality, but also relate to an ever-changing world.

Shared values and diverse projects

The nature of youth culture and youth work is constantly changing. The collaborative investment approach instils the values needed to navigate through these changes, while retaining some sense of personal vision and passion for the work. The YMCA George Williams College course trains workers and underpins these values – reflection in action, trust in workers, freedom in practice, dialogue as a form of evaluation. The Rank network demonstrates them in its attitude and relationship with the workers.

The consistent approach encourages workers to work in the same way through their agencies and with young people. And this is how the philosophy becomes sustainable – a way of working is shared across the partnership. In many cases workers become managers, and Gap year volunteers (or 'Gappers') spring up from the agencies, who then enter in to this relationship with Rank, which further promotes the ethos. And the ripples continue from the 'pebble in the pond'.

Whilst the core values remain the same, there is a huge diversity amongst the workers in whom Rank invests in people of different ages, backgrounds, different types of agencies and across the length and breadth of the country. There is an appreciation that there is no 'one-size-fits-all' model for youth work. Indeed, Rank's strength comes from the diversity of the projects that it supports.

> *Growing your own youth workers. Communities have had too many people who have parachuted in, and then left those communities more confused than when they arrived.*

The investment sows a seed into the community and establishes a commitment from the agency to working locally. Workers are grown in the community.

The Rank network comprises a group of diverse individuals united with the same ideals – the belief in young people and the confidence to trust them and the passion that goes beyond the programme plan to dare to hope for realised potential in the lives of young people and their communities.

Celebration and fun

There are many occasions when we can celebrate the achievements of young people, and rightly so, but the opportunities for us to celebrate the achievements of workers and funders are rare. Rank's positivity is a refreshing approach in the field of youth work, or education.

This sense of celebration is shared throughout the *Youth or Adult?* initiative. Regular conferences allow space for informal networking, as this is recognised as an important part of maintaining good relationships.

Journeying together represents a celebration of all that has been achieved in the last 22 years. This sense of achievement and celebration allows us to feel positive about youth work and a sense of pride in the profession. In my experience, this is rarely reflected outside of the Rank network.

The challenges

> *Has the project changed the organisation? . . . the catchphrase 'the pebble in the pond' has taken root. The ethos has spurred me on.*

> *We started off with a 'Gap' worker and have gone out and found funding for people we identify with a 'spark'.*

The 'pebble in the pond' effect is the best metaphor for Rank's far-reaching impact through an investment, which puts such faith in youth workers and helps them to reach their potential in the communities they love. The philosophy is sustained, as workers in training work to the same ethos and values. They learn to apply the same trust invested in them to the young people they work with.

In terms of a sustainable philosophy for development, there are some key ideas and principles from the Rank experience that can be brought into wider use. The key challenges to be addressed across the board, from front-line workers to policy makers include:

- **Allowing time:** there are no short cuts. Gaining the confidence of young people – especially marginalised young people – takes time. This needs to be reflected in the planning at all levels. Once that confidence has been gained, there may still be a long road to travel before they are willing and able to make significant changes in their lives. It becomes problematic when funders are looking for short-term gains in narrowly defined areas.

- **An approach to risk:** accepting a level of risk (the risk of not achieving goals, rather than in terms of personal safety) releases two vital areas of potential. First, it encourages creativity and imaginative approaches to problem-solving. In addition it creates a learning environment. The phrase 'we learn from our mistakes' is a cliché, because it is true. Unfortunately, there seems an increasing unwillingness to enable people to learn!

- **Being part of a network:** effective work with young people does not happen in isolation. It is vital that the young people are part of a community . . . .and it is also vital that there is a community of support for workers – within their own organisation and beyond. Learning can be exchanged and support found through such a learning community.

- **Evaluation through relationship:** 'the numbers game' is increasingly being recognised as an inadequate way of assessing work within communities. Managers, agencies and funders have to develop ways in which they can maintain a closeness and understanding with young people and workers, in order to better understand and evaluate the impact of informal education.

- **Consistency of approach at all levels:** perhaps the key distinguishing factor of the approach described on these pages is the way all partners aim to work to values and principles that are at the core of good practice in informal education. Building that consistency – from face-to-face work to policy-making – is the single biggest challenge for anyone interested in the informal education of young people.

Questions for reflection

- How do you take into account the time needed to establish trust with young people? What other factors influence the amount of time required to develop youth-oriented programmes?
- What risks (excluding health and safety risks) would you like to take in your work with young people? What are the blocks to this – and how can you minimise them?
- What support do you receive from (and give to) a wider community of practitioners and others involved in informal education? Where do you see potential for further support?
- What alternatives to 'the numbers game' have you identified in your work? . . . are there additional strategies you would like to build?
- Where do you see consistency – and inconsistency – between your face-to-face work, your organisational climate and your relationships with funders? Are there any aspects you would like to address?

CHAPTER 9

Growing a network

Zareena Abidi-Sheldon

In this chapter I want to consider the importance of, and the responsibilities associated with, being part of networks of practitioners. This seemingly ordinary and everyday human activity is a fundamental part of the work. Having a range of connections can help achieve work and personal goals, especially when other resources are limited; and make possible collective activity.

I want to explore the place of networks in generating informal learning, making contacts, exchanging ideas, developing work and, wider still, the opportunity to impact on society, including changing political and social policy. In the first part, I will look at some initial theories connected to networks and networking. In the second, I explore a network in use and, finally in the third, summarise how to get value out of being involved in networks. I draw on my personal experience and, more significantly, the experiences of workers and managers in the network that is the focus of this book. Through discussions and a series of workshops the evidence collected culminated in identifying key aspects of networks and networking, as well as some limitations.

Networking has become a buzz word that is now used in an everyday vocabulary. There are a number of different aspects of being involved in networks or having experiences of networking, which have had an impact on me both personally and professionally. I can think of many examples recently of how I have used the term:

> *I went to the networking meeting.*
> *I didn't get much out of the conference, as it wasn't relevant to my agency, but the networking was useful.*
> *As a new member of staff, it's important to network with colleagues from other areas.*

When I first became a *Youth or Adult?* worker and member of the Rank network in 1997, I was with an agency where I had to work over a wide geographical area and with a large turnover of young people over a very short period of time. When mixing with other new workers and 'older' network members, I discovered that the vast majority worked in the complete opposite situation to me – with small, continuous groups in local community centres, church groups etc. However, at that same event, through *networking* I discovered one person from Scotland who worked in the same style as me. I remember to this day us both standing viewing a map of the UK on the hotel wall and comparing geographical areas.

I can recall the reassurance and relief felt by both of us in finding a connection and correlation in our work, as we had both previously felt quite isolated. It also created an allegiance, as we were able to explain 'together' the nature of the way we worked. The relationship started from this point, becoming peer support and learning and turned into a long-lasting friendship. Throughout our journey together we became confident to question whether the agencies 'worked with young people' or did 'youth work'? On a more philosophical level we were able to acquire an alternative model of the world of work and our individual place in it. In other words, we were able to take different systems, and methodologies of learning, and implement them within our own agencies.

Network theory

For many social theorists, the idea of 'network' is appealing because it can be mapped and measured. But what is it about networks that they figure so prominently within community and voluntary sectors? When people are asked about 'what the word network means to them', they will often refer to intimate social networks such as family and friends. Beyond that perimeter lie work place, church, neighbourhood, civic life and an assortment of other links (Putnam, 2000).

The term 'network' seems to have been first used within social theory by Radcliffe-Brown in 1940 – and its usefulness, in terms of understanding social living, was picked up by sociologists (notably Warner and Lunt, 1942 and Bott, 1955) (Gilchrist, 2009: 47). John Barnes (1954) in an oft-quoted paper, described a social network as a 'set of points some of which are joined by lines. The points of the image are people, or sometimes groups, and the lines indicate which people interact with each other'.

In other words, networks are, essentially, webs. Within them there are nodes (in our case various people, groups, and organisations) that are linked together in some way. Some nodes will have lots of linkages, others one or two. The linkages may be active, strong and significant for the individual, group or organisation; in other situations they may be weak. Using this basic set of understandings, we can map networks and examine the interactions of daily life and think about community dynamics and our place within them (Gilchrist, 2009: 47).

Theory in this area developed out of attempts to explore the compositions and purpose of networks and the part they play. One route was through Gestalt approaches to human psychology and individual behaviours, which, as Scott (1991) has noted, included interactions with others in the social landscape.

In an especially influential contribution Kurt Lewin (1936) used the notion of a 'field' in which 'forces' shape social environments and influence individual behaviour, perceptions and attitudes. Early studies of networks looked at patterns of social interaction and the informal relationships which existed. This was used to appreciate the significance of networks within organisations and neighbourhoods. Gilchrist (2009: 50) notes this process generated a number of useful theoretical developments in the social sciences, notably in sociology, anthropology and organisation theory. These included areas around leadership, trust, decision-making, coalitions and creativity, all of which are relevant to community development and social cohesion. More recently, the perception of networks as a form of organisation has increased in popularity. This is both as an illustrative means, and as a figure of speech.

Networks tend to function on the basis of *informal associations* as opposed to official roles. Membership tends to be voluntary and participative. Collaboration between members relies on influence and reciprocity, rather than compulsion or contracts. As such, networks can be a means of organising communal action, supporting the activities of practitioners, and providing important means of communication.

The rise of social networking websites, such as Facebook and more specialised sites around particular interests, hobbies and work areas, has further popularised the notion of the network. It has also opened up a range of opportunities beyond the sorts of face-to-face interaction that interested earlier researchers. However, with this can also come a more individualistic or self-serving orientation. 'Networking' becomes seen as a means of individual advancement. It entails cultivating contacts or 'working the room' in order to gain a better position or to make money.

A further consideration, as with any grouping, is the extent to which networks exclude different people. It might be that certain people because of how they are seen or who they know, either do not become members of a particular network, or if they do, the relationship between them and significant members is weak. Access to resources, and to influence, may well be restricted as a result. Networks retain considerable power as a form of organising in diverse and often chaotic settings – and it is vital that we attend to issues around access and exclusion.

Networks and social capital

Theories of social capital tend to share the principal idea 'that social networks have value'.

> Just as a screwdriver (physical capital) or a college education (human capital) can increase productivity (both individual and collective), so too social contacts affect the productivity of individuals and group (Putnam, 2000).

Social capital does not have a clear and undisputed definition and the term lends itself to multiple definitions and interpretation (Portes, 1998). However, for the purpose of this chapter I have found that Putnam's definition is of most value:

> Whereas physical capital refers to physical objects and human capital refers to the properties of individuals, social capital refers to connections among individuals – social networks and the norms of reciprocity and trustworthiness that arise from them. In that sense 'social capital' calls attention to the fact that civic virtue is most powerful when embedded in a sense of network of reciprocal social relations (Putnam, 2000: 19).

In other words, interaction by individuals enables people to build communities, to commit themselves to each other and to achieve mutual goals. People can use their social capital to gain access to skills and knowledge in a variety of ways (Field, Schuller and Baron, 2000).

Social capital theory also highlights questions around the direction that a network takes. Putnam (2000) for example, argued that social capital could be *bonding* (or exclusive) or *bridging* (or inclusive). He argued that the former may be more inward looking and tend to reinforce exclusive identities and homogeneous groups; the latter may be more outward-looking. It may also include people across different social divides (Putnam, 2000: 22). To bonding and bridging social capital, Woolcock (2001: 14) has added *linking social capital*. This:

. . . reaches out to unlike people in dissimilar situations, such as those who are entirely outside of the community, thus enabling members to leverage a far wider range of resources than are available in the community.

When considering networks we need to explore the balance between these elements. However, we also need to consider the impact of each. For example, John Field has explored the relationship of social capital to lifelong learning.

At the most general level, the strength of social bonds may shape general attitudes towards innovation and change, as well as determine the capacity of particular groups to survive external shocks or adapt to sudden changes in the external environment. Yet while it is possible that the relationship between social capital and lifelong learning is mutually beneficial, it is equally conceivable that the relationship could be negative. Strong community bonds might reinforce norms of low achievement, for instance, and over reliance on informal mechanisms of information exchange may reduce the demand for more formal and systematic forms of training and education (Field, 2005. See, also, Field and Spence, 2000).

Exploring the possibilities of networks for practitioners

Through networks, the encounters and relationships practitioners have with others from different geographical areas, backgrounds and experiences may stimulate members to learn to question their beliefs and practice. They can link people with others working in parallel; and to those who are like-minded – sharing values and principles. Such networks help to create and sustain what Jean Lave and Etienne Wenger (1991) have described as 'communities of practice'.

Being alive as human beings means that we are constantly engaged in the pursuit of enterprises of all kinds, from ensuring our physical survival to seeking the most lofty pleasures. As we define these enterprises and engage in their pursuit together, we interact with each other and with the world and we tune our relations with each other and with the world accordingly. In other words we learn.

Over time, this collective learning results in practices that reflect both the pursuit of our enterprises and the attendant social relations. These practices are thus the property of a kind of community created over time by the sustained pursuit of a shared enterprise. It makes sense, therefore, to call these kinds of communities 'communities of practice' (Wenger, 1998: 45).

I now want to concentrate on the community of practice that is the focus of this book. Within it from the start was an acknowledgement on the part of the funder of the idea that learning was at the heart of change.

When The Rank Foundation's *Youth or Adult?* Initiative started in 1987 there was an interest in managers and the workers from the different agencies meeting up to analyse the operation of the initiative, and to share learning and practice (support for the Initiative and the approach was also to come later from another Rank Charity – the Joseph Rank Trust). As the Initiative developed, exploring work and questioning routine methods became an additional focus to the usual business of encouraging agencies to develop a clear understanding of what they were doing and what was expected of them. This was helped by the fact that the vast majority of workers trained with the same college (YMCA George Williams College) and through encouraging links between agencies and involvement in Initiative events). It quickly became clear that the emerging network acted as a communication channel, a 'grapevine' that let people know what was going on and drew attention to public events and campaigns. It then began to be seen as useful in mobilising people to take part in collective activity of all kinds and to learn from their own and others' experiences.

There was a change in these members' behaviours and experiences of being involved in the network. I can give two examples at this point based on research gathered from individuals within the network.

First, no longer did members, on the whole, view being part of the network as an administrative task. It became seen more and more as a place to develop their own, and others, practice and perhaps create opportunities for influencing policy change.

Second, the relationships that have developed, and the belief of many of those involved in the forms of community-based youth work that Jon Jolly and Sarah Lloyd-Jones discuss in the opening chapters, have meant that individuals feel attached, i.e. connected. This has been fundamental to sustaining a particular professional identity. A feeling probably intensified by the recognition that the network provides one of the few settings within the current policy and funding climate where the focus is on locally defined youth work, and there is little or no pressure to meet centrally determined targets. Indeed, it is one of the few sites outside of colleges and universities where practitioners can engage critically with youth work and community learning and development.

The potential of the network became more strongly recognised and it began to use its 'connectedness' to work together collaborating on issues surrounding youth work, in order to make change possible. As a result such activity has helped produce a number of publications, CDs and DVDs on key issues affecting youth work, communities, management and organisational issues. Indeed, the production of this book has been a network activity – with the writers (all members of the network) working with practitioners in the network (some 120 in all) to generate material. I was, thus, able to pose a selection of questions to members to gain an understanding of what they perceived their involvement with the network to be; what their expectations were of the network; as well as who they saw as responsible for the maintenance and development. Through working groups, we were able to discuss experiences and examples of involvement and practice on:

- Collaborative working.
- Individual responsibility in promotion, involvement and growing a network.
- The implications and responsibilities related to being involved in a wider body.

The answers were very interesting in that the main general opinions and feedback of members were that:

- There was general commitment and excitement about the possibilities of making a difference and effecting social change.
- Due to the usual barriers – time constraints, lack of focus beyond set events, geographical, financial and logistical issues – it was hard to get anything organised if there was *no-one to organise it for them*.
- Many felt passionately about being involved with the Rank youth work network, as the network didn't just meet for meeting's sake but had focus, positive action and ideas for growth and development.
- Individual learning opportunities were available for workers, managers and agencies.

The main point of learning from this research was that, although the agencies and individuals had much respect for, and involvement within, the events and conferences supported by The Rank Foundation, for anything further to happen on most occasions it needed to be led by an individual or a group.

The membership of the wider Rank youth work network highlighted and created the need for an internal network to support and develop its growth, progression and sustainability. This coincided with a desire on the part of the Foundation to encourage the development of the 'network' to spread an appreciation of home-grown, organically-produced solutions to local problems and the needs for young people and the wider communities. The result was the establishment of stronger underpinnings for the network including a steering group, virtual learning environment and an increased range of workshops and events exploring different aspects of practice. The new framework was called *yarn*.

The establishment of *yarn* entailed a degree of formalisation – but, importantly, this was approached in the same spirit by the funder as in its support of local agencies. Studies of community and voluntary organisations indicate the importance of social networks in their formation and maintenance and yet this is often overlooked by funders (Milofsky, 1988; Chanan, 1992). Neighbourhood and local networks, which are committed to voluntary participatory democracy, can be 'forced' to develop organisational hierarchies to gain support from funding bodies. Through a variety of cultural and institutional pressures such as guidance and funding criteria, network organisa-tions find the need to operate in the same format. They choose to converge by adopting dominant working practices such as bureaucratisation and professionalisation of staff (Milofsky, 1988). Importantly in this respect, the Rank Foundation and Joseph Rank Trust valued and looked to local solutions and, thus, were aware of the issues around convergence. They actively sought to contain pressures to bureaucratisation (both within local agencies, and in the Initiative). The professionalisation of staff was a central objective within the Initiative. However, the form it took placed a strong value on dialogue, and upon building practice from the ground up.

Milofsky further argues (1987) that the survival of individual formal organisations is less important than the development of networks which can hold 'organisational intelligence' and support a pool of local activities, which can respond to particular opportunities or challenges as they emerge. This is a theme which is echoed by Chanan:

> . . . there is a tradition of informal and ad hoc forms of action which from time to time mobilise those people who are more aware of a problem or those who are directly involved . . . they give rise to a social dynamism which fuels the action of the associations even if they are not given any organised or permanent expression (Chanan, 1992).

Some funders have recognised this and sought to support 'DIY community action': 'informal groups of people, acting on a voluntary basis, working together to solve common problems by taking action themselves, and with others' (Richardson, 2008: 1). Many do not. In a world where market ideologies have become dominant and have infused all areas of life, there is a real sense in which we have increasingly lost a sense of working together to make change (Bauman, 2001: 3). Even the tenuous nature of network connections makes it awkward to refer to network membership as if it were a defined category.

How do you get value of a network?

Networks allow members to form clusters to undertake specific activities. These are often focused around a common goal, and coordinated locally. Tarrow (1994) and others have underlined the importance of such personal networks in building and maintaining effective social movements. Examples here include the Civil Rights Movement in America in the 1950s and the Suffragette movement in Britain. Opp and Gern (1993) when researching the protest movement in East Germany prior to reunification, found that the mobilisation of protest was linked to friendship groups, rather than membership of formal organisations. More recently, we have seen the use of social networking and micro-blogging sites such as Facebook and Twitter to organise (for example in the aftermath of the Iranian presidential election in 2009, when discussion of allegations of fraud was not easy elsewhere).

Social development comes about through collective action and learning: combining skills, effort and resources in order to achieve a common goal. This involves working with people, working with structures, and working to change context. The most important and useful aspect of a network, when making judgements about the extent to which people can flourish within them, is its pattern of connections. These often reflect an underlying value base, a shared interest or simply the geography of overlapping lives. Broadly speaking, a network can be regarded as a complex system for processing and dissemination information, which both widens and deepens what we can achieve. The dual purpose of a network is that it enables people to communicate and co-operate around common issues or concerns as well as existing to simply to enjoy one another's company on a social basis!

So what can networks offer practice? For this section I intend to stay with the example of the Rank youth work network. I would like to suggest that a constructive, functional and valuable network format is one that can foster:

A dedicated space to explore practice

There are few forums for workers these days to review and analyse their youth work practices with likeminded individuals. This is mainly due to changes in youth work (and community learning and development) provision, time management, and work pressures within agencies. As such, the relationships and responsibilities within The Rank Foundation network have changed. Previously, youth directors gave a significant input to drive forward the ethos and philosophy of The Rank Foundation. In recent years, its members have been increasingly keen to take part in developing practice, to learn from and share experience with their peers and to gain knowledge on the network and how they can progress within it. Advocacy is one role adopted by the network's members.

An involved and friendly atmosphere to encourage participation

There has been a concentrated effort to create space and persuade individual contribution. For example, at recent conferences participants have been sent in advance of the event, tasks to complete, questions to consider, examples and photos of practice to be presented. In other words, they come along to the conference or event with an expectation of work to do! It is no longer expected that they can turn up and wing it! There is now a strong record of collaborative working that takes place within the network.

Identification and connectedness with the network

Agencies and individuals involved in Rank Charities' activities have been part of growing a solid 'Rank ethos', which has been discussed in the previous chapters. For example, there is an effort to tell others about the work. Within the network there appears to be an increasing wish and need to impart the nature of the work and the lessons realised to policymakers and other funders. This could be said is due to the changes in the direction of youth work and the constraints within which agencies function.

The growth of expertise

As there are a number of agencies, workers, managers, trainees and college tutors within the network, there is a huge pool of resources, knowledge and skills for members to make contact with. It amounts to a considerable body of practice-wisdom.

Conclusion

We have seen that networks are part of a process of encouraging workers and managers within agencies to become proficient in generating their own change. It was Donald Schön who provided an influential theoretical framework linking the experience of living in a situation of an increasing change within the need for learning. He stated:

> We must . . . become adept at learning. We must become able not only to transform our institutions, in response to changing situations and requirements; we must invent and develop institutions which are 'learning systems', that is to say, systems capable of bringing about their own continuing transformation (Schön, 1973: 28).

The professional commitment of individuals and agencies that promote equality and empowerment within networks connected to youth work and community learning and development can play an important part in making 'learning systems' happen. By helping to tackle prejudices and encouraging social development people can use these networks as an opportunity to develop a more equitable flow of information and resources. Why is this required? As in anything in life, people tend to be more effective and enthusiastic when they understand why they are doing things. It is the nature of the relationships between people and the social networks of which they are a part of that is often seen as one of the more significant aspects of 'network'.

Networking is hard work! Good networking is good business! Whether you are a self-employed professional, ambitious to succeed in your career or wanting to make a difference for young people in your local area, the 'need to know' and 'need to be known by' could be considered an essential skill. Networks matter – it's as simple as that. They are being recognised and encouraged as part of a new survival strategy which enables an individual or agency to access work, resources and opportunities. They also create a sense of community and rapport and allow you to share experiences with like-minded people.

The development of The Rank Foundation network has without doubt created a 'connectedness' amongst its members and has over the 20 or more years of the *Youth or Adult?* Initiative encouraged its members to flourish. The network has recognised that the important part being members of social networks play, whether directly or indirectly, in the formation and maintenance of community and voluntary groups. It has itself grown to be a living thing and has become adept at listening to and learning about what its members need individually, as an agency, as a community and as a constitution. The Foundation was able to make the point that 'officialising' its network through *yarn* was a critical point in developing the network. It is an unusual approach from a national funding body and has helped to sustain and develop ways of working relevant to local communities.

Questions for reflection

- What networks are you part of? How significant are they to you?
- Look at a work network involving work with a group of young people or with colleagues. Draw a network diagram – identifying the nodes and the strengths of the relationships. How significant are you to the network?
- Is there one area of activity that you are involved in that could benefit from development as a network? What work would this entail?

CHAPTER 10

Supporting and facilitating long-term change

Chris Dunning

This chapter reviews how an independent funding organisation can support the growth of passion and potential in people working in communities. It is written from the perspective of a member of the executive team at The Rank Foundation.

I argue that the key lies in establishing a way of working as a funder that is consistent with the values of informal learning. The chapter examines both the underlying values of such an approach and the practicalities of putting those values into action.

Introduction: the challenge of consistency

The workers and managers who have contributed to this publication have all received funding through the Rank Foundation's *Youth or Adult?* programme. Central to Rank's approach to funding is a commitment to consistency. The Foundation aims to work with fundees according to the same principles and values it expects of the youth work practice in which it is investing (see box for a summary of Rank's definition of good practice).

Good practice in youth work

The practice that the Rank Foundation is working to promote is founded on the belief that there is good in all. The job of the youth worker is to reach out to that goodness in young people and to create environments where it can grow and be expressed.

Youth work is, at heart, about **relationship** and **association** – connecting and being with others – and the good that can flow from this. Youth work involves:

- Building **relationships** that allow young people to grow and flourish.
- Creating **spaces** with the chance to reflect, learn and grow.
- Enabling **opportunities** to join together to organise and take part in groups and activities.

Having an impact
The Foundation's strategy for creating long-term change in communities is to invest in and support individuals and agencies to become 'pebbles in the pond' – to have a growing influence on their communities over time. This funding strategy has spread its influence through:

- **Growing our own** educator/leaders.
- **Developing ambition** as individuals and organisations.
- Changing our **communities**, principally from within.

For more on Rank's ideas on good practice in youth work, see the booklet that accompanies the *Journeying together* DVD – downloadable from rankyouthwork.org.

Translating the values and principles of good practice in youth work into good practice in funding requires an approach that goes against many conventions. In the development of *Youth or Adult?*, the Foundation:

- **Takes a long-term perspective.** Changing the lives of marginalised young people, from any background, takes time; this is something of which face-to-face workers are very aware – but this reality is rarely reflected in funding patterns.
- **Sees the investment in fundees (individuals and organisations) as starting a relationship,** rather than engaging in a transaction. Rather than, in effect, 'buying' certain outcomes or products, the funder is committing to 'journeying together' – focusing on a professional process, not a pre-determined outcome.
- **Takes a facilitative approach to leadership.** The funder has a leadership role and responsibilities but, as with workers in the field, the method is to draw out solutions from the participants, rather than to define them in advance. Problems and solutions are locally-defined.

There is a definite element of **risk** in this approach. We recognise that it is based in trust and faith in people. Our practice, however, addresses this concern. Specifically:

- The role played by the YMCA George Williams College is central to maintaining discipline and structure to the partnership process, through its approach to the education of professional 'workers with people';
- We have built up over time a sophisticated infrastructure of systems, checks and balances, in order to maximise the effectiveness of the funding programme.

The practical implications of these key characteristics of Rank partnerships are examined in more detail in this chapter.

Long-term investment in people and organisations

Change that is 'rooted', change that is sustainable, takes time. Growing the knowledge and professional skills of a youth worker requires a lasting commitment; their work to create change in communities requires the same long-term perspective.

The term 'investment' is vital. The investment is not simply in an individual, it is in the organisation and community in which they are based. Vitally, it is an investment in their professional development, through the YMCA George Williams College programme.

The Rank Foundation is certainly looking for results but, as with most financial investments, we are prepared to wait for our 'portfolio' to mature. Our view, based on nearly 25 years' experience, is that most initiatives in youth and community work take two-three years to begin to build the foundations of long-term change. In years three to five (as with *Youth or Adult?*), personal growth, project development, agency consolidation, network development and community cohesion really begin to take root.

As a funder, taking a long-term, investment-focused perspective makes a lot of other things possible. It brings an enhancement of the worker/trainee's confidence and security; it also means some stability and growth for the community organisation in which they are based – often the existence of the worker/trainee post attracts additional funding.

In our view, the danger in losing the social capital, should a long-developed agency close in a locality, is not only the loss in financial terms, it is the significant stunting of relationships that have taken years to grow.

From member, to worker to manager

The nature of the opportunities available through the Foundation means that we have supported a number of individuals who, when we first had contact with them were members of a youth group. Through the long-term support available, those individuals have 'graduated' from member to student-worker and then moved on into management. And as a manager, that person has brought another young person into the process! We can point to successful managers, with whom we have had a 12-year relationship – from young participant to senior manager and colleague.

Having followed this same investment philosophy for around 25 years, the Rank Foundation has gradually been growing a network of people and agencies with whom they have established sound long-term relationships, mainly through investing funds in their youth work and personal and professional development.

The 'family' of educator/leaders involved with Rank and operating across the UK in a wide variety of circumstances needs to be constantly nurtured and energised and the *yarn* initiative has been established (June 2008) to enable the thread (yarn) of Rank's work to be regularly discussed (a good yarn!) and acted on, through local/regional or national seminars, informal groups and workshop sessions.

Occasionally there are people who, through extended professional dialogue, have established close relationships with no actual funding being required. This consistency of long-term relationships, through good and bad times, brings about a synergy in the partnerships.

Relational, rather than transactional

The relational focus of our strategy is made possible by the long-term perspective we take. Thinking over the longer-term enables us to build closer – and more open – relationships with those we fund.

Nowadays, so much of the work lies hidden beneath a veneer of gloss and spin – fundees telling funders what they think we want to hear. Funders often put in place a comprehensive range of guidelines, forms and themes to adhere to; they pre-define what someone is looking to achieve, rather than asking what the individual or agency's goals might be.

Applicants for funding have become used to having their goals and outcomes defined by funders (particularly central and local government) rather than being challenged to set their own targets and priorities. This 'funding-led' phenomenon can stifle creativity and development in informal education.

The Rank approach is far more personal. We regularly visit local projects and have a connection with the 'front-line' of youth and community work. We are looking for particular individuals who can, by virtue of their attitude, empathy and approach, see life through the eyes of those with whom they work. They need to be able to relate to young people; we, in turn, need to be able to relate to them. The Foundation executive, visiting an area for the first time, use their own intuition and judgement to sense the possibilities and rate the likelihood of success.

Questions, not answers

On one occasion I had invited some 20 representatives from a variety of agencies working with young people to come along to find out how Rank operates.

A large proportion of the time was spent with delegates asking, for example; what I, the funder, thought was good youth work, what age group did Rank have as priority and how much money could they ask for. On each occasion I bounced back the question to the individual, asking what would they describe as good youth work and why, which was their priority age group and why and how much money did they need to carry out the work?

The way in which Rank seeks initial contact is by the submission of a summary of no more than two A4 pages on which the agency describes what the agency has been doing, the how, the why and with what outcomes; where they are up to now and what would they now really like to do, a vision for their work in the community.

Following the event, I only received one reply and after visits, discussions, reflections and research over the following year – the Rank Trustees agreed to invest in the proposal put forward by this one agency.

Initially Rank is looking for people in an organisation who can relate to the people in their own community and remain true to the needs they find there. The process leading up to the funding agreement is about building trust and preparing for a shared journey for both Rank and the agency.

Mirroring the way youth workers work with young people, Rank takes steps towards the applicants. We seek out leaders and educators who have a passion for their work and wish to value everyone equally. 'Journeying together' will include examining the successes and disappointments of their work in the past and 'the good, the bad and the ugly' aspects of operating their organisation. We all have to accept the risk of being honest and authentic.

Facilitative leadership style

Over the last 30 years Rank has focused its resources, through its youth work and education, on leadership by adults working with young people and with nurturing leadership potential amongst the young.

The Directors, whose executive role is to advise the Foundation's Trustees, have begun to develop a process of 'facilitative leadership'. This approach to leadership possibly emanates from the two Directors' backgrounds in the use of the outdoors and drama as media for personal growth and education. Experiential learning is by no means peculiar to the outdoors or drama, but there is a certain poignancy for the individual when learning through the consequences of actions in both media.

Encouraging learning by doing

- Executive team members spend time with 'Gappers', on residentials and on visits. Here, we introduce these young volunteer leaders from the projects in which we invest, to travelling to new places (possibly the first time they have been out of their own 'patch'), and offer new experiences as facilitators, public speaking, film-making, outdoor experiences and meeting a very varied group of other young people. We also work alongside project workers and managers who are invited to assist with the residentials.

- Rank's executive team have made a point of encouraging Trustees to participate in project visits, so they get to see where young people live. A Trustee came to visit a young men's group on the streets of Belfast, spending some time in a community house on the estate talking through their hopes and fears for themselves and their friends. Upon leaving, the young men thanked the Trustee for taking the time to come out to see them and for his genuine interest in their lives. That one meeting had powerful repercussions: the young people gained a great sense of affirmation from the fact that someone they saw as being influential and from 'the establishment' was prepared to come and see them face-to-face; for the Trustee, it was an un-matchable insight into 'youth work in the raw' – the realities that workers are dealing with; it was also a chance for the Trustee to see and appreciate the subtleties of youth work skills in action.

Over many years our role has become increasingly facilitative with both our Trustees and colleagues, the managers who regulate the projects funded, the *Youth or Adult?* workers and the young people they work with. A key part of our role is to facilitate understanding of the work they – and we – do.

Facilitating an understanding of the work

- The executive team developed, organised and led a series of *Celebration of Youth* events operated in the Lake District where 250 young people, managers and workers operated a showcase of youth work over a four-day period: a night club, a youth café, band performances, a newspaper, a fire show, a small scale business preparing and selling fast food, education sessions on detached youth work, health education, substance misuse etc. An audience of 250 was invited over a 24-hour residential period to participate. The age range was from six months to 85 years!
- Trustees can attend the 'Gappers' (young volunteers) residential, allowing them to gauge how the executive team operates – the methodology, approach and process. They also witness the reaction of those young people attending alongside them. The openness has been exceptionally moving and the personal stories have been profoundly challenging to adults' perceptions of young people's experiences and maturity.

In many instances over the last 20 years the Directors have 'journeyed together', using the outdoors with all of the stakeholders separately and in various combinations. Such direct contact has enhanced relationships and shared experience has encouraged mutual insight, whilst celebrating and valuing difference and diversity. Again there is a strong resonance with good youth work practice and principles. We have constantly sought to encourage people to relate to one another and the physical circumstances in which each lives.

Engaging in joint activities

Both Directors have used their knowledge and experience of the outdoor environment to draw workers, managers, Trustees and young people into significant shared experiences in challenging circumstances, often residentially (a particularly powerful tool in youth work). This activity has involved very senior and experienced mountain guides, yacht skippers and leaders who have, in their own right, been taking responsibility for the programmes.

We have not been advocates for individuals, agencies or communities but rather have taken stances which we hope, in our professional judgement, will remain true to the underlying values and vision of the *Youth or Adult?* Initiative.

Providing stability and vision

- One of the main challenges to the progress and development of this work has been when managers or trustees of local projects have changed during the five years. For a student-worker to have to maintain the vision for their work – as well as their studies – when someone new arrives on the scene can be unbelievably difficult! The relationship between projects and the executive team members means that the worker can, and often does, share their fears and worries with them. For example, the loss of the charismatic leader of an outdoor centre in an accident threatened the existence of the project. The executive remained committed to seeing the projects leader's passion for the outdoors continue. The project's trustees rallied the staff, volunteers and young people; the Rank executive worked alongside the staff to steady the progress of this delicate transition. Rank Trustees were reassured about their ongoing investment; the action also allowed time for potential funders to feel comfortable about supporting the vulnerable agency.
- The 12 contributors on the DVD *Turning Points* describe the people who were significant in their lives at a time of crisis or great change. In each case, the Rank executives have been a consistent part of the picture, remaining true to individual and their journey (watch the DVD at rankyouthwork.org).

Facilitative leadership is not merely delegating. There is some implied authority in our role and (we like to think!) wisdom . . . but power is shared in the way we work with our partners. We recognise the reality that Rank cannot do the work (but has some cash) and the agency can get on with the job (but needs funds). We are nothing without each other.

We have described this leading (and learning) process as 'organic'. By this we mean something which is not artificially generated, not forced or added elements but a wholesome human process of socialising, being more at ease, being true to each other and allowing the necessary time to elapse to establish a sense of trust, primarily through dialogue and conversation.

Using authority, sharing power

A Rank executive is part of the interview panel that appoints the *Youth or Adult?* workers into an agency and has right of veto in that selection. In a number of cases young people have also been an integral part of the process. This cannot be tokenistic. In one case, a candidate had not performed brilliantly during the interview. However, the young people on the panel were adamant that they had plenty of experience of his work and thought he had significantly under-performed. They wanted him as their worker, and he had met all the necessary criteria. The Rank executive could have easily over-ridden their views, but chose not to. Ten years on, the 'recruit' is now a senior manager operating a community enterprise in the outdoors.

It is certainly significant that two of us in the Foundation's executive team – who handle the day-to-day links with funded individuals and projects – have been working together for 20 years. As well as offering consistency, this team of two has complementary styles of working. Between us, myself and fellow Director Charlie Harris also have a breadth of knowledge and experience. Put together, this means that we are able to find effective ways of responding to most situations – and can offer each other a different perspective on the challenges we face. With the relatively recent addition of a third member, we are even better equipped to respond to the broadest range of needs.

Managing risk

Risk is part of the work with young people and, thus, an inevitable part of the funding process.

Young people demonstrate risk-taking behaviour at all sorts of times in pre-and post-adolescence. This is as much about self-discovery and testing out situations, circumstances and actions as being just wilfully confrontational, dysfunctional or awkward. Risk-taking is an essential part of any healthy society.

Challenge, adventure, uncertainty of outcome and self-confidence all need to be reflected at personal, organisational and community levels. As Sir Chris Bonington said in the launch of the 'Campaign for Adventure' (sponsored by the Foundation in 2006) in Parliament 'we do not have to do dangerous things dangerously'.

There is an element of risk taken on many occasions with the employment and entry into training and education of the people who commence the *Youth or Adult?* programme. While there is risk, it is managed and minimised in the way the programme works. Two areas, in particular make significant contributions to minimising the risks involved in the Foundation's investment:

- The partnership with the YMCA George Williams College.
- The systems and infrastructure of the Foundation's ongoing practice.

The partnership with the college

The risk, the hope of realising potential, is shared with the YMCA George Williams College, the employing agency and The Foundation. Indeed, the person on the course must realise an element of risk and challenge posed by the youth work and the education alike, as many have had poor experiences of school or have been out of education for significant periods. There are risks in being challenged to look closely at yourself. The programme will inevitably be part of a process of transition – and people can be vulnerable at times of change.

The relationship with the College is one that plays a powerful role in managing the 'risk' inherent in putting faith in people. In addition to the powerful and relevant content of the programme, there are two important ways in which it achieves this:

- As an educational institution it has its own clear **discipline, structure and requirements**.
- **Reflection** is central to the informal education practice the College promotes – and demonstrates in its way of working.

These two factors combine to integrate a rigour into the whole process that makes an immeasurable contribution to the impact of the whole initiative.

Discipline, structure and requirements

Each prospective student will have to meet the entry requirements, which are not about purely the academic potential of the individual. The very nature of the YMCA movement is to consider people in terms of mind, body and spirit. This resonates with the Foundation's approach and over the years has substantially enriched the relationship between the two organisations.

With so many elements being involved in the process, however, **clear boundaries** that identify the various responsibilities and accountabilities are absolutely essential. As in youth work, complex situations often exist and keeping lines of communication and accountability – including an understanding when confidentiality is appropriate – is a fundamental requirement for the youth worker to be effective.

The College interviews separately and independently, with its own expectations, requirements and procedures. However, there is a harmonising of the two agencies' interviews, which a student/worker will undergo. This demonstrates the mutual understanding and trust that exist in the Initiative.

The focus within College programmes is upon students taking responsibility for their own learning and practice. While there is a clear framework for the completion of course work, and for assessment, the management of this is placed with students. It is they who organise the completion of contracts and assessments, and handle their workload. The latter is significant. The programme involves a mix of distance learning, study days and supervision sessions and, as such, is a very flexible form – but it does require a high degree of self-organisation.

The College operates a 'student-centred approach' that empowers the student to remain at the very epicentre of their relationships with other students, colleagues, managers and supervisors. It also means that, as a result, students are able to work on their own initiative and to make things happen in their projects. Crucially, it helps to build a particular culture – one that sees workers as agents, rather than victims, of change.

During the course of the student/worker's five years of study, the Foundation will have access to their work through visits by executives and Trustees, discussions with their agency manager and/or trustees, young people with whom they work through project visits, meetings with College tutors and course and student review meetings and discussions with fellow students and colleagues.

Reflection in and on practice

The fact that the route to full qualification at the College, working and training on the job, takes five years implies a significant journey in itself for the student/worker. Students will experience an entirely personal journey with colleagues attending study days, supervision, residentials and their own study time.

Distance learning is demanding and requires a careful and disciplined balancing of work and study. This journey has a major input around reflective practice and pushes the informal educator towards a greater understanding of themselves as educators and leaders.

The ethos of the College places a strong emphasis upon developing people's ability to think on their feet – to reflect-in-action (Schön, 1987). Through reflection-on-action stimulated by activities, such as supervision, working with peers, journaling and writing project reports, students develop the ability to think about what is going on in situations and about their own responses and interpretations. These processes and the insights they kindle can be carried into new situations, and help workers to respond to what people are bringing to them. When it is linked to the focus on the worker acting and making change this becomes a powerful force. It both grounds workers in practice – and looks to concrete, local change.

Foundation systems and infrastructure

The Foundation's working practices, developed over time, also add structure and maintain quality within the initiative as a whole. There are a number of key elements:

Visits

There will be engagement with an applicant even before an application is considered by Rank Trustees. Directors' visits are carried out without prejudice, genuinely wanting to know what is taking place and how an agency operates. It is, however, the responsibility of the Trustees to make the decision about whether or not to recommend a financial investment; the Directors' role is to research and advise.

Once a project is financially invested in by the Foundation, a Trustee would expect to visit at an appropriate time. Visits from Directors and Trustees help to re-affirm the expectations, relationships and professional integrity of the active network of projects linked to the Foundation.

The proposal

The written proposal, the main element being the project two-page summary and budget, plays a significant part in the decision-making process. It needs to convey the ability of the people within the agency to grow an experienced but unqualified youth worker and provide evidence of a vision. This relies heavily on the quality and commitment of the people involved and the Trustees must make a judgement on what they can invest in with the finite financial resources they have.

For projects that are not supported financially, the Directors still try to assist them to find funding elsewhere. On occasions, projects bring back proposals for further consideration. The Foundation does, therefore, have the characteristics of a 'place of acceptance' – something synonymous with good youth work practice. We wish to share ideas and vision, operate in good faith and fellowship, establish trusting relationships, take calculated risks in all matters and indeed to enjoy the process.

Status of worker

The *Youth or Adult?* scheme has had to establish clear boundaries. For example, The Foundation does not employ the student/worker, this is their agency's responsibility. However, The Foundation needs to be assured that fair employment and recruitment procedures are in place. As part of this, a member of the executive team will sit on all interview panels for *Youth or Adult?* workers. Should elements of the appointment be substandard, the executive will work with agencies and encourage other agencies with which The Foundation has links to assist, if necessary.

Heads of Agreement

The Foundation has a Heads of Agreement document, which lays out the practical parts of their investment such as finance, payments, training and college matters, conference attendance, evaluation, results and reporting back, policies and regulation. The document is signed by both parties.

Handbook

Each person receives the Agency Handbook (Rank Foundation 2009a), which outlines the Foundation's expectations of all involved and the systems in place. The guidelines have been built up over the lifetime of the whole *Youth or Adult?* Initiative. The Handbook gives practical guidance on how projects are expected to work within the Rank network and the necessary requirements. In effect, it represents the combined knowledge or wisdom gleaned from the past and it is added to and refined every year.

Residentials

Within the first few months of a project commencing, agencies will attend a 24-hour residential event, alongside all other new projects. Representatives from the College and The Foundation will attend as well as some experienced past-funded project managers and student/workers.

The programme uses the Handbook as its 'agenda' and covers key elements, including selection, appointment, college requirements and finances. Towards the end of the 24 hours, each project has time to look ahead 12 months and to share this with colleagues.

A similar event, the six-month follow up event, takes place to allow agencies and the newly appointed student/workers to review progress and re-affirm relationships in the network. The Foundation's administrators attend these events, so that the vital communication between projects and Rank have a face and a relationship for the future. Occasionally a Foundation Trustee attends.

Trustee involvement

While the Foundation's Directors advise, the decisions and the responsibilities rest with the Trustees. Their willingness to engage with the process and the whole approach outlined here is, ultimately, the reason for the programme's longevity and success. They, too, have shared the journey.

The Trustees are certainly not 'yes' people; they have to be accountable and responsible in their decision-making. They must be continually convinced that the long-term investment approach is having an effect.

The directors have acted as 'go-betweens', enabling contact between the Trustees and the individuals, agencies and communities in whom we are investing. This direct human contact is an essential way of demonstrating the impact of the approach to those who have to make the vital decisions.

Trustees regularly visit projects directly, they attend Network events and agency residentials, as well as being part of the governance of *yarn*. They get a chance to talk to the individuals they are supporting – and the individuals get to know them as people, not just as signatures on an official form. All of this exchange helps to sustain the way of working – and is consistent with our underlying goal of consistency between the way we work as funders and the work we aim to support.

These events allow people to reflect on their practice as youth workers and managers. Sharing issues and observations about progress begins to form the interrelationship between people in this sort of youth and community development work.

The yarn *network*

In the last two years, *yarn*, the *Youth or Adult?* network has been established, to link together all those engaged in the Rank investment. The sharing takes place both digitally, via the yarn website, and through meetings at events around the UK.

Each year a September national event is held to bring together all those agencies currently funded by The Foundation to focus on topics of interest to the network. The Foundation's policy on its youth work has been scrutinised and agencies have used the event as a platform for promoting their work.

yarn has a steering group made up of a cross-section of managers, workers, trustees and executives. The College plays an active part in the process of determining the programme and opportunities for learning from the network. Managers will have to balance their 'Rank' work with their other responsibilities, but they can access the network at anytime.

Long-term impact

Our way of working as a funder relies on the consistent growing of relationships and the association of people with similar values. In a world of constant change and indeed increasingly rapid change, the need for constant points of reference becomes increasingly important.

Making a difference

The long-term vision does have the potential to form both shorter and longer term impact on individuals and agencies. In the mid 1980s the Foundation began to invest in an agency that would not normally be perceived to be a youth work organisation, the National Trust (NT).

The basic vision was to appoint a worker through the *Youth or Adult?* initiative to enable access to the wealth of NT's properties and estates by a previously disengaged section of Society who were very unlikely to engage with Heritage. Liz Fisher has worked within the NT and over a significant period of time, over 20 years, and has risen up through the organisation to be a Regional Director. In recent years the NT has reviewed its work and has included the element of 'Community' into its mission statement.

There has been significant personal development for Liz but so too has the agency itself. The potential to achieve change and to make better use of its resources is very significant and there seems to be a strong likelihood that someone within the agency has had a part to play in effecting this change.

The sequential approach of the Foundation's Gap Scheme and Rank Youth Workers' Apprentice Programme (YAP) and Bursaries allows for consistent contacts in local settings.

The Foundation, the agencies and the College invest considerable resources in nurturing what could be termed 'significant positive people' in communities across the UK. There is also a passion for providing 'significant positive events' in a myriad of settings and media, such as theatre, travel, adventure, sport and media, to mention just a few.

This way of working was described in 2002 by Andrew Muirhead (then CEO of the Lloyds TSB Foundation Scotland) as Rank being more 'relational' than 'transactional' when compared to similar independent funders in the same field. He also observed that Rank seemed to 'punch above its weight' in Scotland, when comparative charitable spending was considered between the two funders, intimating that the influence of Rank's work might not only be due to the amount of spending but something else . . . possibly as a result of being 'relational'.

Bringing a huge diversity of people together to discover a common humanity and recognising the essential need for leaders and educators amongst us is the Rank Charities' purpose. As expressed in our respective logos, The Rank Foundation and the Joseph Rank Trust aim to be both a 'pebble in the pond' and 'seed corn' for the future.

Questions for reflection

- In what ways do your relationships within your organisation and with your funder reflect the nature of your relationships with young people? Is there anything you could do to make them more compatible?
- What are the opportunities for making your funding and organisational relationships reflect the nature of the relationships you aim to nurture with young people and across your local community?
- What are the blocks – and the opportunities – for moving your funding towards a relationship, rather than a transaction?

Conclusion

Alan Rogers and Mark K. Smith

We are at a moment when fundamental choices need to be made in the way we, as a society, think about youth work – and education and welfare more generally. The banking crisis of 2008 – and its aftermath – has, to an extent, brought things to a head. However, we have known for some time that there are some key long-term problems. In this conclusion we highlight two of these; and reflect on the lessons for policymakers and funders that can be learnt from the Initiative that has been our focus.

Over a sustained period of time, the Rank Foundation has looked to grow local work and workers – and the experience offers a powerful and engaging alternative to many current, and we suggest problematic, models of approaching the problems and potential of local communities.

The scope and scale of the issues facing us, and the uncertainty and dangers involved, mean we are at a turning point. There are major questions around the economic, environmental and global sustainability of many of our ways of life (Stern, 2006). Furthermore, material advancement is now failing to improve well-being in richer countries – especially that of young people (Layard and Dunn, 2009; Wilkinson and Pickett, 2009; UNICEF, 2007). Against this background, many public services are failing to do what we need of them; and there has also been a weakening of local networks, voluntary organisation and trust. Both have profound implications for youth work, and education and welfare more generally.

The problem of public services

The banking crisis of 2008 has underlined what was already understood by many – there has been a decline in the power of national governments to direct and influence their economies, especially with regard to macroeconomic management. The spread and connectedness of production, communication and technologies across the world – what is often referred to as 'globalisation' – has meant that what happens in local neighbourhoods is increasingly influenced by the activities of people and systems operating many miles away. People and systems are increasingly interdependent (Castells, 1996; Mulgan, 1998).

Something else has been happening. While there have been large increases in government expenditure on certain areas of education and welfare they have not produced results on the same scale (see, for example, Wanless et al., 2007 on health service reform). What is more, there have been a number of reports of front-line workers experiencing declining job satisfaction and feelings of becoming increasingly enmeshed in bureaucracy. An example of this is social work where, as Hilton Dawson (2009) has commented, 'Social workers are under incredible pressure from the volume of records and data that is required by local authorities'. A study funded by the Economic and Social Research Council that examined everyday front line work in five local authorities in England and Wales, raised serious questions about whether 'well-intentioned, modernised systems may actually have compromised the conditions in which good practice can flourish' (White et al., 2008).

This situation has been compounded across education and welfare services by increased central control both over the focus of work (often through the use of targets) and how it is conducted (via commissioning and other means). It has undermined an ability to respond in ways that address local needs and concerns. It has also led to 'playing the system' and created a 'culture of compliance'. Here the problem is threefold.

First, the policies that are being required to be followed are often not properly based in evidence, nor are they doing the job they are supposed to do. Compliance with something believed to be admirable, as Robin Alexander (2004: 22) has argued, 'does not guarantee that it is. And a culture of compliance reinforces policies and practices, good or bad, but cannot test them . . . Compliance is ultimately tautologous'.

Second, as Seddon (2008: 10) has commented, public-service workers have increasingly 'been 'cheating' their systems to meet their targets'. Such 'cheating' or 'gaming' has become ubiquitous and endemic (ibid.: 97). One aspect of this is the way in which, what is in effect lying, eats away at the integrity of front line workers (Smith and Smith, 2008: 142–4).

Last, the way in which third sector organisations and groups are supported by the state is causing problems. Many current funding arrangements, often linked to commissioning, turn groups and organisations into an annex of the state – leaving little degree of discretion for front line workers (Leather, 2007; NCVO, 2007).

Unfortunately, the introduction of market thinking and more commercially-oriented management thinking into public services has also not been without problems. The issues have not come so much from an increased emphasis upon management i.e. the more effective use of resources, but from the models that have been introduced. A basic mistake has been made – 'to assume that management should be the same in all forms of organisation; that in effect management is undifferentiated' (Stewart, 1992: 27). Further, as Michael Sandel (2009: 75–102) has pointed out, markets when introduced into healthcare, education and military matters have unforeseen consequences. They are not neutral and distort – often subtly – the areas they enter. He asks 'are there certain virtues and higher goods that markets do not honour and money cannot buy?' (op. cit.: 102). Market solutions can work against the very things that are being sought. For example, it is not uncommon to find local neighbourhood organisations having to compete against each other in order to secure funding or a contract from a local authority and, in the process, undermining a key policy objective around community cohesion.

The weakening of local networks and organisations

A growing focus on consumption and upon material things has been made worse by a mounting individualism (Halpern, 2010). There is a greater emphasis on the pursuit of individual rather than group goals, and a more instrumental view of relationships (Lane, 2000; Layard, 2005). At the same time there has been a linked decline in many countries in tolerance and trust, membership of informal social networks and in community involvement – what some social scientists call 'social capital'. This is noteworthy as we know, for example, that people living in communities where there are strong networks – and where they are able to join in with activities – are more likely to be healthier, to feel safer (there is less crime) and to prosper (Putnam, 2000; Halpern, 2010). People's happiness depends on the happiness of others with whom they are connected (Fowler and Christakis, 2008).

In the United Kingdom there has been a downward trend over the last thirty years in 'traditional' forms of social capital, such as regular involvement in religious groups, participation in community groups and local voluntary organisations, and the membership of political parties and trade unions. Levels of volunteering have dropped (DCLG, 2009). However, this pattern of change has been complex. For example, in a number of local areas participation in Muslim, Pentecostal and, more recently, Roman Catholic worship has increased. In youth work, whilst there appears to have been a decline in the numbers of locally-based secular organisations, there has been a growth in work associated with churches and religious groups (Nurden, 2010) and this has been reflected in the changing make-up of projects involved in Rank Charities' initiatives.

Different forms of networking have emerged, most notably via the internet. Unfortunately, their nature means that they are no substitute for the sort of concrete support and benefit that local networks offered.

Social change has taken a different form in some countries. For example, social trust has increased in Scandinavia. It seems that whilst in the United States and United Kingdom there has been a move towards people living more private lives, in Scandinavia the response has been more convivial. David Halpern (2009: 10) has described this as follows:

> In essence, we Anglo-Saxons have spent the past few decades using our growing personal wealth to escape from the inconvenience of other people. To use an everyday example, we buy several TVs so that even our own children don't have to negotiate with each other about what to watch. We use our wealth to ensure that we can do what we want, when we want to. In contrast, our Scandinavian neighbours seem to have used their wealth to see more of one another – to go out with friends, to join more reading groups and so on.

When considering this we also need to recognise that people still look to their local communities. For example the English and Welsh Citizenship Survey for 2008–9 (DCLG, 2009) found that 77 per cent of people felt they belonged strongly to their neighbourhood and this represented an increase on 2003 (70 per cent). People also tend see their community as relatively cohesive.

Looking to the local

In the light of such criticism, and with major constraints on public spending, there is increased interest from within all the major UK political parties in the potential of handing more power over services to local government and to citizens. Inevitably there have been different emphases and orientations (see, for example, Cameron, 2009; Byrne, 2009). However, there has been some recognition that social capital and community cohesion can be fostered by increased local citizen involvement and by seeking to strengthen the sorts of groups and organisations that have been at the centre of the youth work initiative that has been our focus in this book.

Such localism, while having a range of benefits, is also not without its problems. It does little to solve fundamental problems, such as those concerning fiscal deficits and income inequality. It may also be that the individualism we have discussed here will take a long time to change. That said it is clear that local alternatives are needed if we are to address the deep-seated issues that are affecting many young people and local communities.

First, and perhaps most obviously, lasting change can only be achieved by engaging with people rather than acting on them. Policy for those deemed marginalised or disadvantaged (such as young people) and for poor communities has tended to be driven by a deficit model, 'that focuses on the deficiencies of individuals and communities, rather than building upon the individual, associational, and institutional assets and networks that already exist' (Sirianni and Friedland, 2001: 11). In contrast, the Initiative that has been our focus here has looked to local individual and associational assets and networks and sought to invest in them.

Second, there is evidence that significant social innovation comes disproportionately from smaller groups and organisations. What is more, the impacts of such innovation are often not the result of organisational growth. Rather, they come from 'encouraging emulators, and transforming how societies think (with new concepts, arguments and stories)' (Mulgan et al., 2007: 2).

Third, investing in local activity and community self-help can, as Liz Richardson (2008: 250–1) has shown, result in triple benefits: improving mainstream services, generating neighbourhood renewal, and reviving democracy.

It is for these reasons that local community, mutual and voluntary organisations must be given more space and resources to fashion policy agendas and to develop locally relevant solutions and opportunities. This entails changing the way resources and services are organised, and moving away from the current ideologies such as commissioning. It means looking to investment. And these are areas in which the Initiative that has been our focus has something powerful to say.

Growing work and workers in local communities

The roots of the success of the *Youth or Adult?* Initiative lie in its underlying values – and the way they are put into practice. It is an approach that:

- Looks to the local identification of needs and the generation of local responses.
- Organises around investment.
- Appreciates workers and fosters their development.
- Approaches the work as 'a pebble in the pond'.
- Operates on a human scale.

These elements link together to form a coherent programme for action both in terms of deepening opportunities for young people and building community.

Starting – and staying – with local agencies and locally-identified needs

One of the defining features of the *Youth or Adult?* Initiative is the way in which it looks to local people to identify needs, and to design 'youth-friendly' projects that address them (see Chapters 1 and 2). Unlike most other funders, The Rank Charities have approached local communities with an open agenda. They have asked local groups and organisations for their analysis of local life and issues – especially with regard to the experiences of young people; and about what they could do, with help, to improve things. There is no set application schedule to fill in for funding. Rather groups and organisations were invited to set an agenda for change, and make the case for a particular project – and how they could support it.

The result has been the development of a wide range of projects and schemes including: young people's building projects, youth cafés, circus and arts ventures, mobile rural youth clubs, innovative church-based work, street and detached work, outdoor and adventure projects, volunteering and enterprise initiatives, and environmental and farming ventures. These have been located in a variety of organisations – many of whom had a long history of local engagement. Others were either recently formed or new to the area of work. Examples of the latter include housing associations and environmental and conservation organisations. One or two of the initiatives worked across quite large areas (especially those located in rural settings) but the vast majority have been neighbourhood-based.

This appreciation of local knowledge and local organisation has resulted in some important gains. First, it has generally created a strong local investment in the project. This can been seen both in the numbers of volunteers involved in many of the projects, and in the way in which other local organisations and groups have become involved. Second, it has meant that projects could have a focus relevant to the neighbourhood or area, and be tailored to work in ways that connected with those concerned. Third, because projects often involved workers and volunteers who were part of neighbourhood or area networks, there could be a direct development of social capital, and an important 'role model effect'. In some of the more deprived communities where projects were based the example of local people making a difference both to their own lives and to those of others led people to become involved or to make their own way into things like training and further education.

Looking to long-term investment

The Rank Charities have focused on investment within this Initiative – on providing agencies with the right resources to grow the work. In doing this they have looked to the long term (five years or more over the first twenty or so years of the Initiative). There has not been pressure to demonstrate short-term gains, but rather to develop work that has quality, substance and sustainability. Such a commitment to support has enabled projects to build a foundation, which – experience has shown – is the basis for significant long-term change and development (see Chapter 3). However, it is not simply the length of the commitment that has been significant – it is its nature.

Crucially, attention was not on immediate returns – but on creating benefits in the future. Furthermore, it was people that were being invested in – young people in particular neighbourhoods or areas, and the youth workers that worked with them. The profit involved was *prōfectus* – progress or advancement. From the start there was a wish to move away from the notion of grant-giving. The concern was not to bestow a favour or gift; not to operate at arms length. Rather it was to work alongside people in local agencies to develop environments and activities that would benefit those involved. More recently, the approach has been experienced as a direct contrast to commissioning. It was not about specifying and buying services, but rather asking those at the front line what they needed to develop.

Adopting 'investment' as an organising idea has also allowed for risk. Some individuals or projects can be seen as reasonably 'safe bets' and used to balance speculating on others (with the possibility of generating innovatory activity, and opening up opportunities for those often denied them).

Placing commitment, reflection and professional development at the core

Speculation is also present in another form. The Initiative has been characterised by a strong emphasis upon reflection, exploration and generating responses to situations that offer possibility (see Chapters 4 and 5). In part this has flowed from a recognition that the commitments, understandings and personalities of workers lie at the core of practice. Good workers need discernment and dedication, as Larry Parsons (2002: 7–8) put it, if they are to discover the 'spark in each of their charges, to look for the talents we all have in some measure'. He continued, 'Having discovered it, educators need to nurture it very carefully until eventually it can be fanned into flame'. Discernment is also fundamental, as we have seen in recent child abuse cases, to safeguarding the well-being of those that workers come into contact with. The focus on reflection and exploration has also assisted with the growth of what could be described as evidence-based or rather evidence-informed practice (Hammersley, 2007). However, the orientation was less to do with making research the basis for practice, than working to make practice the basis for research (Elliot, 2007: 86).

The culture of reflection, commitment and development within the Initiative has in part been created by the involvement in projects, and the leadership of, the Rank Foundation's directors over a sustained period of time. One aspect of this has been the conscious development of the network through encouraging discussion and joint working, and running various network events and conferences.

A further key factor has been the partnership with the YMCA George Williams College. The College has both trained the vast majority of the workers within the Initiative, and has provided support with publication, evaluation and other network activities. The College places reflection at the heart of its whole approach to professional development and has looked to create environments within which workers can explore and struggle with experiences, issues and questions (see Chapter 7). This has helped to stimulate a culture of exploration across Rank's youth work network. By working with the College to build a progressive framework of professional development from Diploma and Access Studies to degree and by investing heavily in training – the Rank Charities have facilitated the growth of high quality local work and a cadre of skilled professionals.

Encouraging agencies and individuals to be 'pebbles in the pond'

The Charities were keen from the start to create environments where able and knowledgeable workers and managers can flourish and 'make ripples' both with those they work directly with, and with others they come in contact with (see Chapter 8). There is a strong emphasis on sharing across the Rank network, and on developing activities with other agencies and groups in local neighbourhoods (see Chapter 9). Workers and managers are approached as change agents whose expertise is grounded in their experience and exploration of practice. The underlying philosophy is that significant and lasting transformations in the field come about, in large part, through direct engagement with good youth work and skilled practitioners – and the ongoing contact within local communities.

Operating on a human scale

As Chris Dunning has written in Chapter 10, 'Bringing a huge diversity of people together to discover a common humanity and recognising the essential need for leaders and educators amongst us is the Rank Charities' purpose'. The Charities have appreciated that relationships are central to all aspects of the work and have thus looked to a facilitative relationship between all partners. There is an emphasis on dialogue; upon talking through issues and discussing questions.

Dialogue, if it is to work well, also requires a relevant structure. Within the Initiative there are far fewer organisational levels than is experienced in many public services; and people at the different levels talk across them. Trustees regularly visit projects and meet with young people, workers and managers. Workers are expected to speak directly to Rank Charities' Directors (rather than going through managers). There is much more personal contact than is the case with many other initiatives (and much less paperwork and reporting). The relational culture brings with it a strong sense of accountability. Those at the front-line are active participants in a culture where giving an account of themselves to all the various stakeholders is agreed to be a good thing. The contrast with the culture of compliance that permeates much recent state intervention couldn't be stronger. Those at the front line are trusted and have discretion. They sustain this by being more open about their work, and being part of a community of practitioners where there is dialogue and an emphasis on doing what is best.

This 'organic' approach also takes into account the reality that projects evolve differently. Flexibility is important. As well as making ripples, local projects inevitably experience turbulence. In order to make sense of changing circumstances they have to adjust what they are doing, and the direction they are taking. One of the features of the Initiative that has been our focus is that considerable discretion is held at the 'front line'. The funder – in choosing to start and stay with locally identified needs, and in looking at funding as an investment – has been ready to entertain and go with major changes of direction.

In conclusion

A simple idea has driven this Initiative: that investing in people to work within their community, while receiving professional training – in this case as informal educators – would bring considerable benefits. It has entailed people 'journeying together' – working together to explore, learn and develop new responses to the situations faced by young people and local communities. The result, as the contributions to this book have shown, is a rich tapestry of practice and an approach that offers considerable potential and possibility.

The practice and approach speak directly to the failure of many public services to do what we need of them; and to the weakening of local networks, voluntary organisation and trust. They also highlight some of the key questions facing policymakers, funders and agencies. Are they ready and able to:

- Look to the local identification of needs and the generation of local responses?
- Organise around investment?
- Appreciate workers and foster their development?
- Approach work as 'a pebble in the pond'?
- Operate on a human scale?

This Initiative – grounded in consistent, long-term work – addresses many of the challenges upon which we must focus if the needs of young people and local communities are to be met. It suggests a fundamental shift in orientation: taking the local seriously; and giving power and discretion to neighbourhood- and community-based groups and organisations. It also shows the power and potential of journeying together.

References

Ackoff, R. (1981) *Creating The Corporate Future: Plan and Be Planned For.* New York: Wiley.

Alexander, R.J. (2004) Still No Pedagogy? Principle, Pragmatism and Compliance in Primary Education. *Cambridge Journal of Education*, 34: 1. [http://robinalexander.org.uk/docs/camb_jnl_article_04.pdf. Accessed November 12, 2009].

Bailey, N. (2005) Transformation or Bureaucratisation? The Changing Role of Community Representation in Local Strategic Partnerships in England. *Journal of Civil Society*, 1(2): 147–62.

Ball, S.J., Maguire, M. and Macrae, S. (2000a) Space, Work and The 'New Urban Economies'. *Journal of Youth Studies*, 3: 3, 270–300.

Barker, J.A. (1993) *The Power of Vision Video Cassette.* In Goodstein, L.D., Nolan, T.M. and Pfeiffer, J.W. *Applied Strategic Planning.* New York: Mcgraw-Hill.

Barnes, J. (1954) Class and Committees in A Norwegian Island Parish. *Human Relations*, 7: 39–58.

Beck, U. (1992) *Risk Society: Towards A New Modernity.* London: Sage.

Bauman, Z. (2001) *Work, Consumerism and The New Poor.* Buckingham: Open University Press.

Beem, C. (1999) The Necessity of Politics. Reclaiming American Public Life. In Smith, M.K. (2007) '*Social Capital*', The Encyclopedia of Informal Education. www.infed.org/biblio/social_capital.htm.

Ben-Shahar, T. (2008) Positive Psychology. Talk at *Go Dundee.* http://www.godundee.co.uk/events/tal-ben-shahar/. Accessed November 27, 2009.

Beynon H., Hudson R. and Sadler D. (1994) *A Place Called Teeside.* Edinburgh: Edinburgh University Press.

Bolman, L. and Deal, T. (1991) *Reframing Organisations: Artistry, Choice and Leadership.* San Francisco: Jossey Bass.

Bolman, L. and Deal, T. (2008) *Reframing Organisations: Artistry, Choice and Leadership.* 4th edn. San Francisco: Jossey Bass.

Bott, W. (1957) *Family and Social Network.* London: Tavistock.

Bourdieu, P. (1979) *Outline of a Theory of Practice.* Cambridge University Press.

Bourdieu, P. (1986) The Forms of Capital. In Richardson, J.G. (Ed.) *Handbook of Theory and Research for The Sociology of Education.* New York: Greenwood Press.

Bourdieu, P. (1989) Social Space and Symbolic Power. *Sociological Theory*, 7: 14–24.

Brainwaremap (2009) Holistic Learning. *Brainwaremap*. http://www.jwelford.demon.co.uk/brainwaremap/holist.html. Accessed October 21.

Brooks, R. and Goldstein, S. (2001) *Raising Resilient Children*. Chicago: Contemporary Books.

Burns. D. and Taylor, M. (1998) *Mutual Aid and Self-Help. Coping Strategies for Excluded Communities*. Bristol: The Policy Press.

Bynner, J., Ferri, E. and Shepherd, P. (1997) *Twenty-something in the 1990s: Getting on, Getting by, Getting Nowhere*. Aldershot: Ashgate.

Byrne, L. (2009) *Radicals With Realism*. Speech to Institute of Government, November 12, *Liam Byrne, Labour MP for Birmingham Hodge Hill*. http://liambyrne.co.uk/blog/radicals-with-realism-my-speech-on-public-servie-reform/. Accessed November 13, 2009.

Cameron, D. (2009) *The Big Society*. Hugo Young Lecture, November 10, *Myconservative.Com*. http://www.conservatives.com/news/speeches/2009/11/david_cameron_the_big_society.aspx. Accessed November 13.

Castells, M. (1996) *The Rise of The Networked Society*. Oxford: Blackwell.

Catan, L. (2004) *Becoming Adult: Changing Youth Transitions in The 21st Century. A Synthesis of Findings From The ESRC's Research Programme: Youth, Citizenship and Social Change 1988–2003*. Brighton: Trust for The Study of Adolescence.

Chanan, G. (1992) *Out of The Shadows: Local Community Action in The European Community*. Dublin: EFILWIC.

Children's Society (2009) *A Good Childhood*. http://www.childrenssociety.org.uk/all_about_us/how_we_do_it/the_good_childhood_inquiry/report_summaries/13959.html.

Cohen, A.P. (1985) *The Symbolic Construction of Community*. London: Tavistock.

Cooperrider, D.L. (1999) *Appreciative Inquiry: A Positive Revolution in Change*. San Francisico: Berrett-Koehler..

Covey, S. (1999) *Principle Centred Leadership*. London: Simon and Shuster.

Cowen, S. (2003) *Foundation of Faith: A History of The Rank Foundation*. Lewes: The Book Guild. http://www.rankfoundation.com/histobj/.

Cresswell, T. (2004) *Place: A Short Introduction*. Oxford: Blackwell.

Crow, G. and Allan, G. (1994) *Community Life: An Introduction to Local Social Relations*. Hemel Hempstead: Harvester Wheatsheaf.

Davies, B. and Gibson, A. (1967) *The Social Education of The Adolescent*. London, University of London Press.

Dawson, H. (2009) Baby P: One Year On. *The Guardian* November 11. http://www.guardian.co.uk/society/2009/nov/11/baby-p-vox-pops. Accessed November 11, 2009.

De Botton, A. (1998) *How Proust Can Change Your Life*. New York: Vintage International.

Department for Children, Schools and Families (2008) *Reducing The Number of Young People Not in Education, Employment or Training (NEET): The Strategy*. London: DCSF.

Department for Communities and Local Government (2009) *Citizenship Survey: April 2008 – March 2009*. London: DCLG.

Department for Education and Skills (2002) *Transforming Youth Work: Resourcing Excellent Youth Services*. London: DfES.

Dewey, J. (1897) My Pedagogic Creed. *School Journal*, 54: 77–80.

Dewey, J. (1933) *How We Think*. New York, DC: Heath.

Doyle, M.E. and Smith, M.K. (1999) *Born and Bred? Leadership, Heart and Informal Education*. London: YMCA George Williams College/Rank Foundation.

Dweck, C.S. (2006) *Mindset. The New Psychology of Success*. New York: Random House.

Edwards, M. (2004) *Civil Society*. Cambridge: Polity.

Elliot, J. (2007) Making Evidence-Based Practice Educational. In Hammersley, M. (Ed.) *Educational Research and Evidence-Based Practice*. London: Sage.

Elsdon, K.T. with Reynolds, J. and Stewart, S. (1995) *Voluntary Organisations. Citizenship, Learning and Change*. Leicester: NIACE.

Erikson, E.H. (1995) *Childhood and Society*. London: Vintage.

Evans, K. et al. (2003) *Taking Control: Young Adults Talking About The Future in Education, Training and Work*. Leicester: National Youth Agency.

Field, J. (2005) Social Capital and Lifelong Learning. *The Encyclopaedia of Informal Education*, www.infed.org/lifelonglearning/social_capital_and_lifelong_learning.htm. Accessed October 20, 2009.

Field, J. (2008) *Social Capital*. 2nd edn. London: Routledge.

Field, J. and Spence, L. (2000) Social Capital and Informal Learning. In Coffield, F. (Ed.) *The Necessity of Informal Learning*. Policy Press, Bristol.

Field, J., Schuller, T. and Baron, S. (2000) Social Capital and Human Capital Revisited, in Baron, S., Field, J. and Schuller, T. (Eds.) *Social Capital: Critical Perspectives*. Oxford University Press, Oxford.

Fowler, J.H. and Christakis, N.A. (2008) Dynamic Spread of Happiness in A Large Social Network: Longitudinal Analysis Over 20 Years in The Framingham Heart Study. *British Medical Journal* 337: A2338. http://www.bmj.com/cgi/content/full/337/dec04_2/a2338. Accessed November 11, 2009.

Freire, P. (1972) *Pedagogy of The Oppressed*. Harmondsworth: Penguin.

Frost, P.J. (2007) *Toxic Emotions at Work: And What You Can Do About Them*. Boston: Harvard Business School Press.

Furlong, A. (1992) *Growing Up in A Classless Society? School to Work Transitions*. Edinburgh: Edinburgh University Press.

Gadamer, H-G. (1979) *Truth and Method*. London: Sheed and Ward.

Geertz, C. (1983) *Local Knowledge. Further Essays in Interpretive Anthropology*. New York: Basic Books.

Giddens, A. (1999) Risk and Responsibility. *Modern Law Review*, 62: 1, 1–10.

Gilchrist, A. (2007) Working With Networks and Organisations in The Community. In Deer Richardson, L. and Wolfe, M. (Eds.) *Principles and Practice of Informal Education, Learning Through Life*. Abingdon: Routledgefalmer.

Gilchrist, A. (2009) *The Well-Connected Community. A Networking Approach to Community Development*. Bristol: The Policy Press.

Gilchrist, A. and Taylor, M. (1997) Community Networking: Strength Through Diversity. In Hoggett, P. (Ed.) *Ideas of Community*. Bristol: Policy Press.

Goetschius, G.W. and Tash, M.J. (1967) *Working With Unattached Youth. Problem, Approach, Method*. London: Routledge and Kegan Paul.

Goodstein, L.D., Nolan. T.M. and Pfeiffer, J.W. (1993) *Applied Strategic Planning*. New York: Mcgraw-Hill.

Green, A. and White, R. (2007) *Attachment to Place: Social Networks, Mobility and Prospects of Young People*. Joseph Rowntree Foundation.

Green, M. and Christian, C. (2002) *Accompanying: Young People on Their Spiritual Quest*. London: Church House Publishing.

Habermas, J. (1984) *The Theory of Communicative Action Volume 1*. Cambridge: Polity Press.

Hall, G.S. (1904) *Adolescence*. New York: Appleton.

Halpern, D. (2009) Capital Gains. *RSA Journal*, Autumn, 10–15. http://www.thersa.org/fellowship/journal/features/features/capital-gains. Accessed November 11.

Halpern, D. (2010). *The Hidden Wealth of Nations*. Cambridge: Polity.

Halpin, D. (2003) *Hope and Education: The Role of The Utopian Imagination*. London, Routledge-Falmer.

Hammersley, M. (Ed.) (2007) *Educational Research and Evidence-Based Practice*. London: Sage.

Handy, C. (1999a) *Inside Organisations. 21 Ideas for Managers*. London: Penguin.

Handy, C. (1999b) *Understanding Organisations*. London: Penguin.

Hawkins, P. and Shohet, R. (2000) *Supervision in The Helping Professions*. Buckingham: Open University Press.

Henriques, B. (1933) *Club Leadership*. London: Oxford University Press.

Heron, J. (1996) Helping Whole People Learn. In Boud, D. and Miller, N. (Eds.) *Working With Experience: Animating Learning*. London: Routledge.

Hodkinson, P., Sparkes, A.C. and Hodkinson, H. (1996) *Triumphs and Tears: Young People, Markets and The Transition From School to Work*. London: David Fulton Publishers.

Holtom, D. and Lloyd-Jones, S. (2008) *Youth Work in Wales: Issues for Policy and Practice in The Future*. Welsh Assembly Government.

Howell, W.S. (1982) *The Empathic Communicator*. Belmont, CA: Wadsworth Publishing.

Jeffs, T. (2001) 'Something to Give and Much to Learn': Settlements and Youth Work'. In Gilchrist, R. and Jeffs, T. (Eds.) *Settlements, Social Change and Community Action*. London: Jessica Kingsley.

Jeffs, T. and Smith, M.K. (1999) The Problem of 'Youth' for Youth Work. Youth and Policy, 62, 45–66. Also Available in The Informal Education Archives, http://www.infed.org/archives/youth.htm.

Jeffs, T. and Smith, M.K. (2005) *Informal Education: Conversation, Democracy and Learning*. Nottingham: Educational Heretics.

Jeffs, T. and Smith, M.K. (2008) Valuing Youth Work. *Youth and Policy*, 100: 277–302.

Jeffs, T. and Smith, M.K. (2010) Introducing Youth Work. In Jeffs, T. and Smith, M.K. (Eds.) *Youth Work Practice*. London: Palgrave.

Jones, G. (2002) *The Youth Divide: Diverging Paths to Adulthood*. York: York Publishing Services for the Joseph Rowntree Foundation.

Johnston, L. et al. (2000) *Snakes and Ladders: Young People, Transitions and Alternative Careers*. Bristol: Policy Press and York Publishing Services.

Kearns, A. and Parkinson, M. (2001) The Significance of Neighbourhood. *Urban Studies*, 38: 12, 2103–10.

Kenway, P. (2005). *Monitoring Poverty and Social Exclusion in Wales 2005*. York: Joseph Rowntree Foundation.

Kindermann T.A. (1996) Strategies for The Study of Individual Development Within Naturally Existing Peer Groups. *Social Development*, 5: 158–73.

Kouzes, J.M. and Posner, B.Z. (2002) *The Leadership Challenge*. San Francisco: Jossey-Bass..

Kretzmann, J.P. and McKnight, J.L. (1993) *Building Communities From The Inside Out: A Path Towards Finding and Mobilizing Community Assets*. Chicago, IL: ACTA Publ.

Lane, R.E. (2000) *The Loss of Happiness in Market Economies*. New Haven: Yale University Press.

Lave, J. and Wenger, E. (1991) *Situated Learning. Legitimate Peripheral Participation*. Cambridge: University of Cambridge Press.

Layard, R. (2005) *Happiness. Lessons From A New Science*. London: Allen Lane.

Layard, R. and Dunn, J. (2009) *A Good Childhood. Searching for Values in A Competitive Age. The Report of The Good Childhood Inquiry*. London: Penguin.

Leather, S. (2007) Speech to The NCVO Annual Conference Wednesday 21 February 2007, *Charity Commission* http://www.charity-commission.gov.uk/recent_changes/speech.asp. Accessed September 14, 2009.

Lewin, K. (1936) *Principles of Topological Psychology*. New York: Mcgraw-Hill.

Lifelong Learning UK (2008) *National Occupational Standards for Youth Work*. London: LLUK/NYA.

Lin, N. (2002) Social Resources and Social Mobility: A Structural Theory of Status Attainment'. In Fuller, B. and Hannum, E. (Eds.) *Schooling and Social Capital in Diverse Cultures*. Amsterdam: JAI/Elsevier.

Lloyd, C.B. (2005) *Growing Up Global: The Changing Transitions to Adulthood in Developing Countries*. Washington DC: National Academies Press.

Lloyd-Jones, S. (2005) *A Map of Transition in The South Wales Valleys*. Phd. Thesis, Cardiff: University Of Wales.

Luthar, S.S., Cicchetti, D. and Becker, B. (2000) The Construct of Resilience: A Critical Evaluation and Guidelines for Future Work. *Child Development*, 71: 3, 543–62.

MacDonald, R. (2002) *Youth, the 'Underclass' and Social Exclusion*. Routledge.

MacDonald, R. and Marsh, J. (2005) *Disconnected Youth? Growing Up in Britain's Poor Neighbourhoods*. Basingstoke: Palgrave Macmillan.

Mahoney, J. (2001) What is Informal Education'. In Richardson, L. and Wolfe, M. (Eds.) *Principles and Practice of Informal Education*. London: Routledgefalmer.

Margo, J. and Dixon, M. (2006) *Freedoms Orphans: Raising Youth in A Changing World*. London: Institute for Public Policy Research.

Mcdowell, L. (2001) *Young Men Leaving School: White Working Class Masculinity*. Leicester: Youth Work Press and York Publishing Services.

McLaughlin, M.W., Irby, M.A. and Langman, J. (1994) *Urban Sanctuaries: Neighbourhood Organisations in The Lives of Futures of Inner-City Youth*. San Francisco: Jossey-Bass.

Miller, R. (2000) A Brief Introduction to Holistic Education. In *The Encyclopaedia of Informal Education*, http://www.infed.org/biblio/holisticeducation.htm. Assessed November 20, 2009.

Milofsky, C. (1987) Neighbourhood-Based Organisations: A Market Analogy'. In Powell, W.W. (Ed.) *The Non Profit Sector: A Research Handbook*. New Haven: Yale University Press.

Milofsky, C. (1988) Structure and Process in Community Self-Help Organisations. In Milofsky, C. (Ed.) *Community Organisations: Studies in Resource Mobilisation and Exchange*. New York: Oxford University Press.

Minton, A. (2009) *Ground Control. Fear and Happiness in The Twenty-First-Century City*. London: Penguin.

Mulgan, G. (1998) *Connexity: Responsibility, Freedom, Business and Power in The New Century* London: Viking.

Mulgan, G. et al. (2007) *In and Out of Sync. The Challenge of Growing Social Innovations*. London: National Endowment for Science, Technology and The Arts.

Murray, C. (1990) *The Emerging British Underclass*. London: Institute of Economic Affairs.

Murray, C. (1994) *Underclass: The Crisis Deepens*. London: Institute of Economic Affairs.

NCVO (2004) A Bed of Roses? *Strategy and Impact*. http://www.strategy-impact.org.uk/page.asp?id=1495. Accessed September 15, 2009.

NCVO (2007) *The UK Voluntary Sector Almanac 2007*. London: NCVO.

National Youth Agency (2004) *Ethical Conduct in Youth Work: A Statement of Values and Principles From The National Youth Agency*. Leicester: NYA.

National Youth Agency (2007) *NYA Guide to Youth Work and Youth Services*. London: NYA. http://www.nya.org.uk/information/108737/nyaguidetoyouthworkandyouthservices. Accessed November 20, 2009.

Nurden, H. (2010) Working With Faith. In Jeffs, T. and Smith, M.K. (Eds.) *Youth Work Practice*. London: Palgrave.

Opp, K-D. and Gern, C. (1993) Dissident Groups, Personal Networks and Spontaneous Co-Operation: The East German Revolution of 1989. *American Sociological Review*, 58: 659–80.

Palmer, P.J. (1993) *To Know as We Are Known. Education as A Spiritual Journey*. San Francisco: Harpersan Francisco.

Palmer, P.J. (1998) *The Courage to Teach. Exploring The Inner Landscape of A Teacher's Life*. San Francisco: Jossey-Bass.

Parsons, L. (2002) *Youth Work and The Spark of The Divine*. London: YMCA George Williams College for The Rank Foundation.

Plas, J. and Lewis, S. (2001) *Person-Centred Leadership for Nonprofit Organisations; Management That Works in High Pressure Systems*. London: Sage.

Portes, A. (1998) Social Capital: Its Origins and Applications in Modern Sociology. *Annual Review of Sociology*, 24: 1–24.

Putnam, R.D. (2000) *Bowling Alone. The Collapse and Revival of American Community*. New York: Simon and Schuster.

Radcliffe-Brown, A.R. (1940) On Social Structure. *Journal of the Anthropological Institute of Great Britain and Ireland*. 70: 1, 1–12.

Rank Foundation (2007) *Turning Points. Twelve Youth Workers, Twelve Stories*. DVD London: Rank Foundation. http://www.rankyouthwork.org/turningpoints/index.htm. Accessed November 26, 2009.

Rank Foundation (2008) *Journeying Together: Youth Work Through The Youth or Adult? Initiative*. DVD Cutts, P., Booklet Rogers, A. and Smith, M.K. et al. London: Rank Foundation/YMCA George Williams College.

Rank Foundation (2009a) *The Agency Handbook*. London: Rank Foundation/YMCA George Williams College. http://www.rankyouthwork.org/agency_support/agency_handbook_2009.pdf. Accessed November 29, 2009.

Rank Foundation (2009b) *The Volunteers' Handbook*. London: Rank Foundation/YMCA George Williams College. http://www.rankyouthwork.org/gap/award_handbook_2009.pdf. Accessed November 29, 2009.

Richardson, L. (2008) *DIY Community Action. Neighbourhood Problems and Community Self-Help*. Bristol: The Policy Press.

Rogers, A. (Ed.) (2005) *Coming of Age. 18 Years of Learning From The Rank Foundation Gap Award*. London: Rank Foundation/YMCA George Williams College. http://www.rankyouthwork.org/publications/coming_of_age.pdf. Accessed November 29, 2009.

Rogers, C. (1967) The Interpersonal Relationship in The Facilitation of Learning. In Leeper, R. (Ed.) *Humanising Education*. Alexandria VA: Association for Supervision and Curriculum Development. Reprinted in Kirschenbaum, H. and Henderson. V.L. (Eds.) (1999) *The Carl Rogers Reader*. London: Constable.

Rose, D. (2004) The Potential of Role-Model Education. *The Encyclopedia of Informal Education*, www.infed.org/biblio/role_model_education.htm. Accessed November 26, 2009.

Rudd, P. and Evans, K. (1998) Structure and Agency in Youth Transitions: Student Experiences of Vocational Further Education. *Journal of Youth Studies*, 1: 1, 39–62.

Sandel, M.J. (2009) *Justice. What's The Right Thing to Do?* London: Allen Lane.

Savage, J. (2007) *Teenage: The Creation of Youth Culture*. London: Viking.

Schein, E.G. (1990) Organisational Culture. *American Psychologist*, 45, 109–91.

Schön, D.A. (1973) *Beyond The Stable State. Public and Private Learning in A Changing Society.* Harmonsworth: Penguin.

Schön, D.A. (1983) *The Reflective Practitioner.* Basic Books: New York.

Scott, J. (1991) *Social Network Analysis: A Handbook.* London: Sage.

Seddon, J. (2008) *Systems Thinking in The Public Sector: The Failure of The Reform Regime – and The Manifesto for A Better Way.* Axminster: Triarchy.

Seligman, M. (2004) *Authentic Happiness: Using The New Positive Psychology to Realise Your Potential for Lasting Fulfilment.* New York: Free Press.

Senge, P.M. (1990) *The Fifth Discipline. The Art and Practice of The Learning Organisation.* London: Random House.

Sirianni, C. and Friedland, L. (2001) *Civic Innovation in America. Community Empowerment, Public Policy and The Movement for Civic Renewal.* Berkeley: University of California Press.

Smith, H. and Smith, M.K. (2008) *The Art of Helping Others: Being Around, Being There, Being Wise.* London: Jessica Kingsley.

Smith, M.K. (1994) *Local Education. Community, Conversation, Praxis.* Buckingham: Open University Press.

Smith, M.K. (1999, 2002) Youth Work: an Introduction. *The Encyclopaedia of Informal Education,* www.infed.org/youthwork/b-yw.htm. Accessed November 26, 2009.

Smith, M.K. (2003) From Youth Work to Youth Development. The New Government Framework for English Youth Services. *Youth and Policy,* 79, Available in The Informal Education Archives http://www.infed.org/archives/jeffs_and_smith/smith_youth_work_to_youth_development.htm. Accessed November 26, 2009.

Smith, M.K. (2005) Parker J. Palmer: Community, Knowing and Spirituality in Education. *The Encyclopaedia of Informal Education.* http://www.infed.org/thinkers/palmer.htm. Accessed November 26, 2009.

Smith, M.K. (2001, 2006) Evaluation. *The Encyclopaedia of Informal Education,* www.infed.org/biblio/b-eval.htm. Accessed November 26, 2009.

Spillane, J., Hallett, T. and Diamond, J. (2001) *Exploring The Construction of Leadership for Instruction in Urban Elementary Schools: Leadership as Symbolic Power.* Unpublished Paper. Northwestern University.

SQW Consulting (2008) *Neighbourhood Management Pathfinders: Final Evaluation Report. People, Places, Public Services: Making The Connections.* London: DCLG.

Stern, N. (2006) *The Economics of Climate Change. The Stern Review.* Cambridge: Cambridge University Press. Downloadable from: http://www.hm-treasury.gov.uk/independent_reviews/stern_review_economics_climate_change/sternreview_index.cfm. Accessed January 8, 2008.

Stewart, J. (1992) Guidelines for Public Service Management: Lessons Not to Be Learnt From The Private Sector. In Carter, P., Jeffs, T. and Smith, M.K. (Eds.) *Changing Social Work and Welfare.* Buckingham: Open University Press.

Sutherland, G. (1990) Education. In Thompson, F.M. (Ed.) *The Cambridge Social History of Britain 1750–1950 Volume 3: Social Agencies and Institutions.* Cambridge: Cambridge University Press.

Tarrow, S. (1994) *Power in Movement: Social Movements, Collective Action and Politics.* Cambridge: Cambridge University Press.

Taylor, M. (2008) *Transforming Disadvantaged Places: Effective Strategies for Places and People.* York: Joseph Rowntree Foundation.

Tett, G. (2009) *Fool's Gold: How Unrestrained Greed Corrupted A Dream, Shattered Global Markets and Unleashed A Catastrophe.* London: Little, Brown.

Tiffany, G. (2001) Relationships and Learning'. In Richardson, L. and Wolfe, M. (Eds.) *Principles and Practice of Informal Education.* London: Routledgefalmer.

Tucker, S. (2005) The Sum of The Parts: Exploring Youth Working Identities in Working With Young People. In Harrison, R. and Wise, C. (Eds.) *Working With Young People.* London: Sage.

UNICEF (2007) *The UNICEF Report Card (2007) Child Poverty in Perspective: an Overview of Child Well-Being in Rich Countries.* Florence: UNICEF Innocenti Research Centre.

Wanless, D. (2007) *Our Future Health Secured?* London: King's Fund.

Warner, W.L. and Lunt, P.S. (1942) *The Status System of The Modern Community.* Newhaven CT: Yale University Press.

Wenger, E. (1999) *Communities of Practice. Learning, Meaning and Identity.* Cambridge: Cambridge University Press.

White, S. et al. (2008) Repeating The Same Mistakes. *The Guardian* November 19. http://www.guardian.co.uk/society/joepublic/2008/nov/19/baby-p-mistakes. Accessed November 11, 2009.

Wilkinson, R. and Pickett, K. (2009) *The Spirit Level. Why More Equal Societies Almost Always Do Better.* London: Allen Lane.

World Bank, The (1999) What is Social Capital? *Povertynet* http://www.worldbank.org/poverty/scapital/whatsc.htm.

Young, K. (1999) *The Art of Youth Work.* Lyme Regis: Russell House Publishing.

Index

Russell House Publishing Ltd

We publish a wide range of books on work with young people including:

Kids at the door revisited
978-1-898924-58-6

By Bob Holman

This book tells the story of a community youth work project in Bath through interviews with young people who were involved. It also tells their stories over the decade that followed.

Its core message must not be overlooked: effective support for young people at risk cannot be built in a vacuum and must be developed organically in the context of the cultures and communities to which they belong.

Young People Now

Having their say
978-1-898924-78-4

Young people and participation

Edited by David Crimmens and Andrew West

*An interesting and informative read for policy makers, professionals and young people themselves, and indeed anyone interested in developing children and young people's participation in **political life**, citizenship and social inclusion.*

Children & Society

Essays in the history of youth and community work
978-1-905541-45-4

Discovering the past

Edited by Ruth Gilchrist, Tony Jeffs, Jean Spence and Joyce Walker

Dedicated to unravelling the many past aspects of youth and community work and providing an anchor for contemporary practice . . . The mix of contributions . . . range from narrative reflection to more conceptual and philosophical analysis . . . focus on both influential people and projects and movements . . . They engage with the wider politics and religion that influenced the development of youth and community work.

Howard Williamson in Youth Work Now

Youth work process, product and practice
978-1-905541-11-9

Creating an authentic curriculum in work with young people
By Jon Ord

Great overviews of the essential elements for good youth work, participation and power, relationships and group work, choice and voluntary participation, methods and experimental learning. So much is missed if we do youth work for outcomes' sake alone.

Youthwork

Ord suggests that: 'Youth work cannot defend itself against erroneous and rival conceptions of practice unless it can sufficiently articulate its own. Through providing a **framework for the creation of authentic curricula for youth work** . . . this book offers one of the means by which individual workers, services and the profession as a whole can promote its unique educational practice.'

Young people in post-conflict Northern Ireland
978-1-905541-34-8

The past cannot be changed, but the future can be developed
Edited by Dirk Schubotz and Paula Devine

Covers not just what we expect to hear when NI is being discussed: violence, sectarianism, faith-segregated schooling, cross-community contact, politics, the peace process. But also: inward migration, mental health, suicide, bullying, pupil participation, sexual health, poverty, class, and how best to find out about these things in robust ways that involve young people in shaping the process.

Radical Youth Work
978-1-905541-57-7
Developing critical perspectives and professional judgement
Brian A. Belton

I have rarely, if ever, ended a conversation with Brian without feeling the interesting discomfort of some surprising new insight. I sense that this book, in its turn, will leave readers with an academic hair shirt of doubt and curiosity. It cannot, necessarily, be a book of answers but nor is it simply one of questions. For me, what makes the book radical is the apparent ease with which the author hands back the thinking to where it belongs for each one of us: to the reader. That is the kernel which reminds us of the enormous and radical possibilities of youth work – the intellectual stance which shares thinking and concluding in a spirit of mutual engagement and effort. It will support work with young people by supporting the workers and by focussing our attention clearly on the fruitful moment where our work blossoms in the light of our thinking.

From the Foreword by Mary Wolfe,
Principal, YMCA George Williams College

Just like a journalist
978-1-905541-46-1
Helping young people to get involved
with newsletters and newspapers
By Suzy Bender with illustrations by Lyn Davies

A clearly written introduction to all the basic issues to be addressed when looking to either produce your own newsletter or to get your material published elsewhere. Youth workers ought to be comfortable with and skilled at both these kinds of involvement. The agenda around promoting young people's voice and influence, and the related issue of combating the negative representation of young people, is compromised if they and those that support them are unable to engage with the media.

Tim Burke in Youth Work Now

Working with Black young people   978-1-905541-14-0
Edited by Momodou Sallah and Carlton Howson

Raises illuminating and critical policy and practice questions for policy makers, practitioners and academics alike.
The Howard Journal

Provides appropriate facts and figures to highlight current issues, concerns and events . . . practitioners, students and trainers should all find something useful.
Youth Work Now

*Addresses relevant topics with **academic rigour and passion**. A publication such as this has been long overdue . . . **a key text***
BJSW

Mixed-up kids?   978-1-905541-38-6
Race, identity and social order
By Tina G. Patel

An excellent book . . . very readable . . . presents some original and thought-provoking ideas . . . a great resource.
Adoption & Fostering

Looks at how increasing numbers of children are growing up in mixed-race families and the influence this has on their lives.
Youth Work Now

Who am I? Who are you?   978-1-903855-93-5
Ideas and activities to explore both your and young people's assumptions, beliefs and prejudices
By Jenny Nemko

With its equilibrium of philosophy and scope for creative ideas, offers necessary breadth to produce good youth work practice, enabling young people to make informed choices and explore their own values, attitudes and spirituality.
Young People Now

The author tackles this huge subject matter in a thought-provoking, concise manner, while not shying away from vital topics and questions.
Youth & Policy

Secret lives: growing with substance   978-1-903855-66-9
Working with children and young people
affected by familial substance misuse
Edited by Fiona Harbin and Michael Murphy

Most books of this genre discuss either how to assess the issue or how to work with it: this book does both, leaving the reader with a sense of confidence as to how they might go about working with this group of service users, as well as why they are working with them in this way . . . I recommend this book for all concerned about substance misuse.

Community Care

Respect in the neighbourhood   978-1-905541-02-7
Why neighbourliness matters
Edited by Kevin Harris

Offers an astute analysis of the nature and effects of 'respect', as it is lived out in the day to day lives of ordinary people, but also points to ways in which it might be sustained and, even more ambitiously, restored.

Professor John Pitts, Editor of Community Safety Journal